On Cuddling

"Antwi invites us to look more closely at the associations between the cuddle, the choke, the hold, and the coffle for Black people. But, beyond the violence of the racial embrace, he also finds a place for fugitive cuddling, the comfort that arcs back and forth between those who flee, those who escape, and even those who remain held back. This book will take its place among others by Christina Sharpe, Saidiya Hartman, and Hazel Carby that have investigated the violence of intimacy and the intimacy of violence."

—Jack Halberstam, author of
Wild Things: The Disorder of Desire

"A necessary book about holding, being held, and the hold(s) of the past. Playful, vulnerable, ever acute—Antwi gets down with the funk of language, history, and bodies to make fugitive sense of modernity as anti-Black grammar and embrace."

—Nadine Attewell, scholar of intimacy,
empire, and diasporic life

"An urgent and elegant text … excavating the many meanings of cuddling under racial capitalism. Antwi's writing is lyrical and powerful; the way he harnesses epistemology and polysemy to build both dancing prose and crucial political analysis is revelatory."

—Sophie K Rosa, author of *Radical Intimacy*

T0284051

VAG ABO NDS

Radical pamphlets to fan the flames of discontent
at the intersection of research,
art and activism.

Series editor: Max Haiven

Also available

001
*Pandemonium: Proliferating Borders of Capital
and the Pandemic Swerve*
Angela Mitropoulos

002
*The Hologram: Feminist, Peer-to-Peer
Health for a Post-Pandemic Future*
Cassie Thornton

003
*We Are 'Nature' Defending Itself: Entangling Art,
Activism and Autonomous Zones*
Isabelle Fremeaux and Jay Jordan
Published in collaboration with the
Journal of Aesthetics & Protest

004
Palm Oil: The Grease of Empire
Max Haiven

005

On Cuddling

Loved to Death in the Racial Embrace

Phanuel Antwi

PLUTO PRESS

First published 2024 by Pluto Press
New Wing, Somerset House, Strand, London WC2R 1LA
and Pluto Press, Inc.
1930 Village Center Circle, 3-834, Las Vegas, NV 89134

www.plutobooks.com

British Library Cataloguing in Publication Data
A catalogue record for this book is available from the
British Library

ISBN 978 0 7453 4611 3   Paperback
ISBN 978 0 7453 4615 1   PDF
ISBN 978 0 7453 4613 7   EPUB

Typeset by Stanford DTP Services, Northampton,
England

Simultaneously printed in the United Kingdom and
United States of America

VĀG
ABO
NDS

Contents

Dedication   vii

Be Held   1
  A Scroll   15
Scene of Subjection, Choreography of Care   18
Racial Embrace   27
Hold. Womb. Tomb. Spoon.   37
  The Dead Can Love Us Too   53
Grammars of the Black Atlantic   57
Bearing   73
Attraction and Abjection   85
  Continuous Present   95
State Cuddling   101
Loved to Death   123
Theater, Hustling, Embrace   136
  It's Almost Time   149
Fugitive (Solidarity (Betrayals))   150

Acknowledgments   161
Notes   166

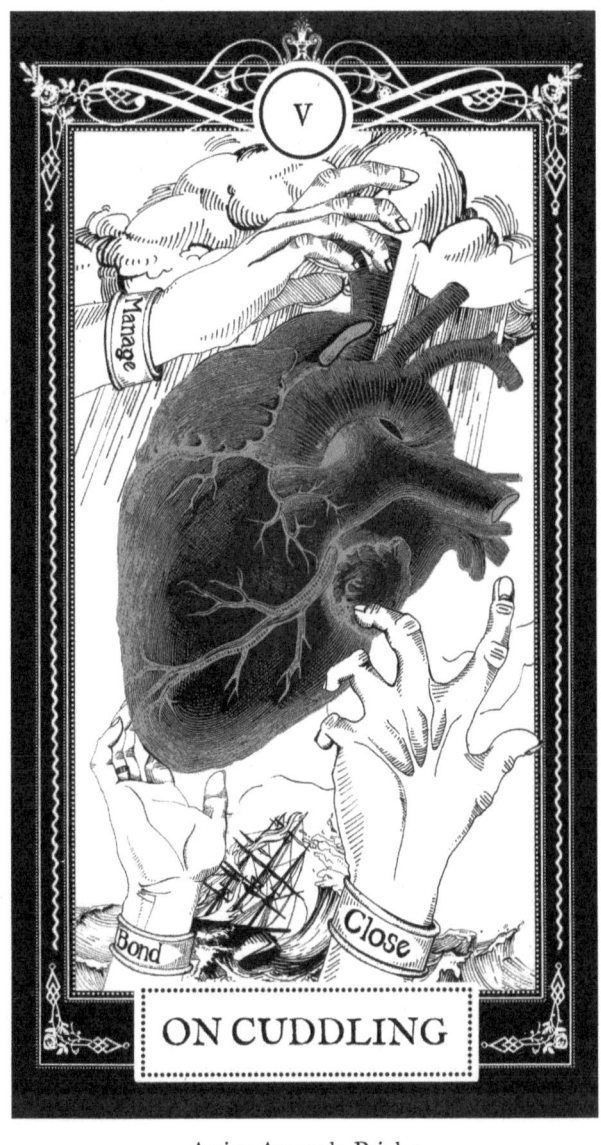

ON CUDDLING

Artist: Amanda Priebe

Dedication

To my parents (my maternal grandmama and grandpapa, and my mom and dad), for everything you did to safeguard my life.

To my sisters, for years of tickles and massages and pinches, all my love.

To those who return, may there be rest in the journey.

Be Held

In which the author informs us of the ways in which cuddling is not only life-giving but death-giving for Black people.

This book on cuddling was written in the uneasy air of pandemic times when, as a grown man, witnessing again and again Black men having the life crushed out of them, I found myself wanting to be cuddled by my maternal grandmama.

It was written from the labyrinth isolation of my apartment in Vancouver. I had moved to the allegedly calm, multicultural Canadian city with a broken heart and broken bones six years prior, in 2014, in a time of uprisings. This moment of brokenness marked the changing conditions of my work and life. Here I was, alone in a new city, working to hold myself together after practicing the art of surrendering the weight of my body into the sensuous folds of another. In the absence of this shelter, without the arms I have learned to surrender myself into, I became vulnerable to two arms of institutional cuddling: the medical profession and the university system, with their "conditional hospitality."[1] Away from familiars and familiar surroundings, not only was I vulnerable to these two arms, I also had to confront the non-neutrality of the racist weather in this new city.

In their suffocating embrace, I imagined myself curled up on my grandmama's lap, or, as she liked to tease me, under her armpit, where the chambers of her body offered passageways to another world, and nightly, even when briefly, she'd teasingly wrapped me in the vestibule of another world. Her lap and armpits, where I was guest and host, gave me a home as big as some of the questions I want to ask about cuddling. Why, for example? And how? And when? Why and how and when does cuddling become murderous? The racial embrace . . . Why and how and when does news of another killing pass over us like an unquestioned weather system, imagined to be inevitable, unremarkable . . .

Christina Sharpe has called the whole, invisibi-lized climate created from and for anti-Blackness "the weather," and it engulfs Vancouver, a moun-tainous coastal city often associated with its low cloud ceiling that mutes the sunlight most days of the year. This was no less the case in 2014, the year that North America swelled with waves of protests against racial violence at the hands of the police. This was a key date, one freighted with "evaluative space to pay attention to the meaning and impact of different scales of action in the process."[2] It was a lively summer of protests. The videotaped evidence of Eric Garner having the life squeezed from him in the devastating embrace of New York Police Department Officer Daniel Pantaleo was everywhere, and protesters everywhere were chanting "I can't breathe," echoing Garner's inaudible last words, into the air. The media loop on Ferguson showed protesters burning down structures of the repressive state, paradoxically broadcasting the strength and fragility of those who cared more for Black lives. On the university campus where I had begun to work, students supporting the #BlackLivesMatter movement were also in solidarity with protesters across the water, in Hong Kong, the Umbrella Movement. Rebellious noise that flowed through Vancouver, where Musqueam, Squamish, and Tsleil-Waututh defended their unceded lands, changed the vibratory skin of the city.

I was far from home in a city whose weather wrapped me too tightly and not tightly enough. When I think about the non-neutrality of the weather, I am also thinking about the concrete features and assertion of the city and my vulnerability to the spiral entanglements in the elemental forces of place: ways that once-familiar winds that caressed my face now tingled my skin, causing me to distrust the profound necessity of my body's sensations. Even though students and activists took to the streets to protest the murders, the general agreement of most Vancouverites was that *this could not happen here*, that these lethal embraces were the exotica of America's exceptional history. And yet the everyday, normalized, embodied experiences of anti-Blackness afforded me no such comfort. I was being told, in a million tiny ways, that this city would never be my home. And yet, at the same time, my university and other institutions in the city turned to me and my Black colleagues, exhausting us with requests to perform a racial meteorology, to explain the anti-Black weather that they, only now, were discovering. Loved to death in this suffocating institutional embrace that demanded answers and that left my bones and my body exhausted, my thoughts returned, again and again, to my grandmama's cuddles and the home it created for my questions.

For many of us, home is a touchstone question, in terms of who we are. For others, cuddling is a touchy question, in terms of boundaries, exclusion, forming a space of interaction and shared subjectivity. Domesticated into a familiar activity, cuddling rarely gets treated as a serious concept that can carry the heavy philosophical and theoretical questions of our time. Aside from a few artists (the arresting cover of Claudia Rankin's *Citizen: An American Lyric* and Adrian Howell's ethical-negotiation performance work, *Held*) and psychologists (who tend to focus on the relational interactions of cuddling in the romantic domain),[3] it is imagined as a passing comfort among animals, or between humans and animals, or experienced as an activity that occurs between mothers and children, or between lovers in the private space of home. And yet, when cuddling offers home, it grows full with questions. What happens when we move cuddling from the private space of the home into the public space of culture and politics, and even economics?

On Cuddling is an invitation to meditate on the practices that go into finding home in each other when there's no boundary that's real, no exclusion that's given, and all of us are part of the same great huddle, past and present and future as entangled possibilities, the overall phenomenon of humanity, messy, violent, loving. Particularly, it invites us to think with the conventional graphics of cuddling but unties its social contracts—its "instituted trace"[4] to comfort and to romance—in order to help us think through the kinds of intimacies that we not only learn but also conform to, or discipline others to conform to, when it comes to (mis)managing Black lives. In other words, I am resisting the object performance of cuddling as a way to insist that the movements of care and vulnerability that some experience as intimacy in cuddling can, for bodies that are exiled by fences of rule, become calculated cho-reographies that get used as weapons to kill. The theatrical acceleration of intimacy that led to the suffocation of Eric Garner and George Floyd, of them being held to death in public by agents of the state invites us to look again at how cuddling, a practice *with a long historical arc and a continuous (hidden) deep structure of danger*, can offer a space to exercise state-sponsored violence.

Initially, I blamed my distrust of the city on which I had to depend but to which I had no relation on its elemental materials: air, land, and water. I was sure the changes to my diet accounted for the shifting morphology in my body sensations. My body was not surrendering to this new place, nor was it positively correlating to the theater of diagnosis through which the medical system was channelling my body and its sensations. In fact, the weekly appointments and revolving blood tests were beginning to induce in me doubt about what I was sensing; my capacity to hold on to the ecological-political forms of violence I believed to be affecting my body was slipping. The structures of care were failing me; they were draining my energies, too. I wanted to escape everything that was happening and, at the same time, I wanted to surrender the weight of everything, including my own weight, into the repeated movements that had once offered me shelter. Choreography is a set of planned movements, intended to be performed over and over again, and cuddling, I will argue, is a choreography. But in this moment, no cuddling choreography could be executed. As a result, I began to refract my interactions with the medical system, the university, and the world around me through questions of cuddling. The result is this book.

Here is some of what I learned: Understood both as a curative and lethal practice, cuddling marks a contradictory site, making it a difficult political art worth engaging. I have, for example, sought to draw a line that connects the infatuation of commercial television with "cuddly" large Black women to what I am calling "state cuddling": the punishing use of seemingly neutral bureaucracy to render a killing form of care. I have sought to link the murderous public strangulation of Black men in the police choke hold to the hold of slave ships. And throughout, I have held tight to how, through queer intimacy, poetics, funk, and fugitive solidarities, we who are embraced by anti-Black violence refuse, and cuddle other possibilities. We are, all of us, locked in the racial embrace, but it does not cuddle us all in the same way.

Readers who wish for the comforts of a declarative politics must, in this book's embrace, prepare themselves for disappointment. Of course, I am committed to refusal, resistance, collective liberation, abolition, rebellion, riot, and mobilization. Our moment requires it. But in this text, I am seeking something more subtle. It is an attempt to grapple with questions: how is/was an anti-Black world being made, past and present? How is that world making all of us? And what can yet still be made of that world? As a poet and a literary theorist who is dedicated to attending to the traces of Blackness where we don't expect to find them, in this book it is my duty to try and unfold these questions as they might be found in the nuance of language, that shared archive. Here, I exercise my literary imagination and apply the tools of literary criticism to economics, social institutions, popular culture and, more generally, to the weather systems of anti-Black violence. Hence the reader should expect the unexpected and also recognize the care with which the words operate in both poetry and prose.

In writing this book, I have had to confront what it means to cuddle death, an idea, a person, and concept, and, in doing so, I have written a book that feels out of line with the way I have come to understand what makes a book a book. Just as the curative practice of cuddling requires a consenting other, *On Cuddling*'s express desire is for its readers to regard the work of reading as a conscious activity of making, one that gets lighter if we read not simply to see ourselves as only we can, but also to open up in each other surprising conversations about dignity; we can have a chance at this conversation if we allow ourselves to see the pages formed as forms still forming. This poetic exercise in reading also marks my writing. To be with an other, compositionally, recalls the montage, so as not to feel trapped in the fragmentary loop from and within which I try to understand a world that keeps chattering.

The loop of murders that work to interrupt my writing informs my formal choices; the fragments of poetics and criticism, of autobiography, philosophical musings, therefore, are not coincidental. It is my vanity to disown the command for integration and acknowledge this conscious craft on behalf of you. I am displaying ways these deaths affect my process, showing their effect on my imagining and thinking. These deaths are not distracting me from the project. These deaths are refractions from the world; these worldly events that keep crashing into me, and my worldly experiences of them as a nightmare mired in the trying presence of now, interrupt my words and my world, informing the controlled uncontrolled experiences that inform this book.

This looping, crashing force (a tidal force that recalls Kamau Brathwaite's insistence we forgo traditional Eurocentric dialectics for *tidalectics* of the Black Atlantic) might also be recognizable in the poetry and prose of this book. When one is forced, as Black bodies are, to live in the *continuous present*, one is asked to embrace grammar differently.

Given the scant conceptual weight typically ascribed to cuddling, and given the amount of baggage that this familiar practice holds for some of us, I have elected to gather familiar objects and events and practices that equally tend to receive less conceptual attention as a way to examine ways that the multiple aspects of our material and desiring lives condition the mismanagements of Black life. These include the making of the teddy bear, a popular image of the slave ship, *Brookes*, a scene from an American reality TV show, *X-Factor*, US economic policy, as well as what might at first appear to be the most trivial details of a number of police murders. I want to stress that just because these extrajudicial killings happen in the United States does not mean the ramifications stay there: the US weather system of anti-Blackness (wrapped around a form of unforgiving capitalism) emerges from the same field of forces that animate the wind and waves around the world. I have chosen, for the most part, to focus on the United States because, for reasons of its empire, all of us global subjects are compelled to become literate in its operations.

Fundamentally, this book on cuddling is also a book about intimacy: intimacy as a way of un/knowing, cuddling as a fleshy epistemology. I long for more ways for all of us to be close, to hold one another, and for a longer period of time, without quieting or rearranging the arc of each other's line. But this book, does not concern itself with the oxytocin many of our bodies release in a cuddle and the ways we might harness it for pleasure, profit or politics. I *do* preoccupy myself with the roles associated with oxytocin: social bonding and reproduction, and the tug of longing their release elicits in relational intimacy (attachments, belonging and home). And what of cuddling and sex (before, during, after, instead of)? Indeed. Let's hold the question tightly even while we do not look at it directly: in this book, it's close at hand.

Yet the association of cuddling with comfort is not the whole story. The perception of cuddling as romantic and friendly gives us only part of the picture. This book explores more coercive and catastrophic cuddles as they subtend Black life and death. As much as we want to think of cuddling as a practice of care, intimacy, and tenderness, we also need to account for ways that care, intimacy, and tenderness are also media of violence. Relationship counsellors, novelists, and theorists will tell us: It is not so uncommon to feel smothered, held down or suffocated by one or ones who claim to love us. However, this book explores what it means to be loved to death by systems, and what emerges, shimmering, squiggling, from killing care.

While I remain interested in intimacy's epistemologies of the cuddle, this book is more interested in the collective fantasies and histories we draw inspirations from when society holds Black people and makes vestibules with and out of our bodies. "Vestibule," another name for porch or entrance depending on whether one favors the seventeenth- or eighteenth-century etymology, is derived from the vestibular system, a major sensory organ we rarely notice until we experience motion sickness or dizziness related to infections of the inner ear and lose our sense of equilibrium and balance. Vestibule's relationship to the portion of the inner ear that controls equilibrium and balance suggests how a vestibule's primary use is to orient us into our position in the world. For many, being held in a cuddle restores balance to our position in the world. It is related to listening, and the listening we do here opens (and I mean to hold open and not foreclose) cuddling's meaning.

Let us dwell with the cultural resonance of "porch," that space of intimacy that sits in your house and in the world at the same time, where people sit, eavesdrop, gossip, watch, and talk. Zora Neal Hurston's *Their Eyes Were Watching God*, rooted in folklore and oral storytelling, understands the significance of the porch as a gathering space for banter, soaking up histories and listening to stories. Here, porch-sitters' ears watch, eyes listen, at times even touch beneath the floors of the porch to encourage and welcome home a storyteller. If we think of cuddling along the sensorial lines of a porch, cuddling as a practice, is an interface of sorts—a tactile mutuality, a non-mirroring tactility, creating a common tactile surface by rhyming shapes and positions, at times mirroring each other's shapes, and through it all retaining an opaqueness to intersubjectivity. The porch is a threshold, an interior-exterior holding. If we think of the porch in terms of cuddling positions, and consider one body as a vestibule for another, cuddling becomes an exterior exteriority that creates interiority, a tactile inbetweeness that is also a mutual inbetweeness rather than the creation of an interior, a place. *On Cuddling* plays with this cultural vestibule and the controlling perception of cuddling as a comforting and relaxing activity rather than also experiencing cuddling as an activity, with concrete opacity. This book will keep beckoning readers into this sense of the porch/ vestibule as a place of convening to suggest that the Black body is itself a porch and vestibule for the Other's body—a community-gathering and equilibrium-restoring place.

And from this vestibule, this place we pause to embrace guests or hosts as we arrive or before we leave, we will be listening to the intricacies of misunderstanding that envelope the cuddle that (mis)manages Black lives. Following the associative compositions and coordination in practices of cuddling, my thinking in this book weaves words to worlds by rematerializing, via defamiliarizing, the referential surfaces in the language of cuddling's many optima (its connotations, associations, and etymologies). This at-times uncomfortable or discomforting approach will allow me to sketch/ stretch out the various registers of "cuddle" I am working with, as well as the adjacent terms it evokes (care, embrace, intimacy), which helps create the condition to hear and feel the dumpy trajectories of the cuddlepoetics that this book aspires to map.

Through citations, I have credited the community of writers whose work, during the isolation of lockdowns, offered shelter and companionship. They were, on some days, the only companions I trusted to hold me without agenda; I held on ambivalently. The lack of movement, or the shrinking of spaces of separation between us as a result of the pandemic, influenced my circulation between genres, making *On Cuddling* a book that embraces open exchange and celebrates collaborative participation. Feeling singular and alone in my apartment in the pandemic, my thinking and writing became highly citational at some points, gesturing to an embrace of sociality.

What, then, has my broken heart got to do with my broken bones, and what does the pain from both have to do with cuddling? While I hesitate to claim brokenness as the surrogacy that gave birth to *On Cuddling*, I will acknowledge that the accumulated pain from both reoriented me to the benefits of lying in a fetal position. I've always figured out how to be grown, however, on those curl-myself-up-into-question-mark days, on days when my search for a place to rest heart and bones yielded no results, the absence of sheltering eyes and hands made me plead with this hang-around pain to allow my body to receive the needle piercing my skin to draw blood as companion. Soon, the harmony of the rhythm beneath the rhythm of this cyclical drama, which is to say, the eye of the needle and the shoulder pat from the lab technicians, became more important than the results the blood work would yield. I embraced these small intimacies. And because I was spending as much energy going to the doctors as I was living with pain, I began to think about Christina Miserandino's theory which uses the spoon as a metaphor to describe the impact that chronic pain has on the daily lives of people.[5] Spooners, Miserandino points out, begin their days with a limited number of spoons, and because every task requires a certain amount of energy, meticulously planning and making difficult choices about how you use units of energy is necessary or else one runs the risk of using too many spoons and likely using up all of their energy and risking crashing. This dispensation of energy started me considering the relationship between spooner and spooning and thinking about the choreographed energies in the cuddle.

Having undertaken this project on cuddling, with its syncopated trajectories, has taught me ways that the aftermath of a loss can spark the genesis of a project. I have grown surer that the work some of us dedicate our lives doing return us to ourselves; or rather, the mundane devotions of our daily lives help us listen to matters of the world. I remain a cuddler committed to pointing out that all of us interested in cuddling are not all cuddled in the same way, by the same arms, by the same institutions.

VAG
ABO
NDS

A Scroll

What we say

ME: You don't understand, *I'm* the one who collects things to give you when we're apart.

YOU: [CRYING] No, *you* must understand, I'm an illusion of solid ground.

How we brought

ME: Uncle Baldwin says, "'*Somebody*,' said Jacques, 'your father or mine, should have told us that not many people have ever died of love. But multitudes have perished, and are perishing every hour—and in the oddest places!—for the lack of it.'"

YOU: Auntie Lorde says, "The true focus of revolutionary change is never merely the oppressive situations which we seek to escape, but that piece of the oppressor which is planted deep within each of us."

WE: The awe of watching sister Denise, that magician, dirty restrictive forms and leave intoxicating matters to their own dirt. Rendering all the fruit and the chaff, her out-way through.

What we do

We continue to put our hands in pockets with sticky pocket pasts in front of us and expect to see what's behind us when what's behind will be changing.

What I dream

The body soil is dense and elastic with waves that move the ground from side to side that up and down as you push and pull through me.

You hover as I sit in a tub, broth steeped in rounds of *what if this* and *maybe that*—where did the crate of mango go? the bottle of scotch?—and time slows and unravels and I cannot lucid myself out of the well.

I see a shirt hugging air on a line I think you'd wear. I know that it is you because you know I don't know what level of purchase I am. Our eyes uproot themselves in their garden.

The earth of your yam-fed lips cuddle mine from a world that means every harm.

How we recall

YOU: You, muttering in your sleep, *she creates potions, she cures with language, the world was never modern.* We, immersing all those bits and pieces of our bodies and minds, bits and pieces not separated from each other in her world, we were apprenticing to be magicians who come to know life without bird-songs without bees without *not enough.*

You refuse to let go of good old days when, as Ali and Mo, we sailed snails back and forth on each other's chest—those readings. I recall more than your v frame (although, lord, help me walk away from the memories of those tight pants with stitched roses on their right front pocket where my hand roamed) that summer.

ME: You, beautiful dishonest you, my opposite, repeal; caught in your loop, I've fueled you.

How else to account for your wavey thumb tipping its tongue on my temple to access hinges in my brain that swing doors; it wasn't long ago you'd rush over after work, curl up to a vinyl record, neck and neck, brown butter, piggyback on Sunday's undecidability, eat pancakes, for dinner, take turns being Frankie's bride. Not Mary's monster: mine took the shape of an Ocean whose kiss was that summer, now a value six earthquake in the yard where my spine tree shakes. Even now, as you beg for understanding, and tell me I've lost our way, you dodge my questions. Take my confession: 'member my shirt you treated negligee? The one when on makes me Black and Black like cardinal; the one I would slip on late nights and crawl into your bed? I know you didn't lose Black Cardinal, the touch-torch ghost of our evenings.

Scene of Subjection, Choreography of Care

In which our author advises that cuddling, which breaks down the learned boundaries of self and other, can embody an investigation of not only those intimacies that bring us home, but also the way some bodies are held fast by systems of domination.

For those of us who do not have a home, a cuddle is often a way of either coming home or finding home. This is not my way of saying that every cuddle is a space of home or a desire for home, nor that the space of a cuddle secures home or comfort. The invitation to cuddle has sometimes presaged betrayal. The embrace can also feel suffocating. And home can be a place of conflict, of threat, of invasion. In fact, home can feel like a kind of warzone, and a cuddle can kill, fast or slow. This is especially so for many who are not allowed to be at home in the empire, or who are confined or incarcerated in or by society: Indigenous people, people of color, people who are disabled, or queer or poor, women, cis or trans: we all are embraced by systems that claim to choreograph our care but make war on us.

What separates (when a separation is discernible) home as a warzone from home as a cuddleplace? Despite the contradictions of the cuddle, and because I am moved by the promise of home as a place where "complex personhood"[6] is granted, I am searching for the meanings of cuddles as one searches for home.

Why cuddling? Because what I am calling the racial embrace is often too close to see, entangled with our sense of self and other, our sense of comfort and care, our sense of belovedness and betrayal.

If a cuddle promises home, then a cuddle is a dense relational field where histories get connected and intertwine. It is a corporeal paradigm for relations, where these histories, like people, touch; where a body re-composes its needs artfully onto and energetically into another body; where the skin we live within offers protection to a self, an other, and becomes a dependable home; where at times it is easy for limbs and other parts to reach across dividing lines, become entangled with other limbs and other other parts; and where, at other times, with arms taut, fatigued by exchange of heat, by the will of home, to cuddle, in one sense, is, to borrow from Lauren Berlant, "to communicate with the sparest of signs and gestures."[7] Amidst this kind of cuddle, a body, any body, can interrupt the intimate trajectory, the energy field, eloquently squirm away from the heart of the embrace to assert its autonomy—the return of the subject's illusory self-sufficiency, that mask of fear of disclosing more of oneself, the refusal of seamlessness. Or one can be beside another's self, tacitly accepting that *I and I alone* am not alone. A head can snuggle into the nook of a neck, at home, not yearning to escape the unstable sign that divides the cuddling I and the cuddled I. We listen with our bodies to feel each stomach growl in melody with breath. Such vibration could turn to eroticism. We might hear, in the length of the growl, a horn sounding the passage of time. In the harmonics: the cry, the joy, the pain, the recalls of memories of past touch, still touching, humming, settling. Such choreography. Yes, there is information in this corporeal entanglement: the wait in stillness and silence, the fragility in meaningful sensation. They inform the adjustments in our shelter; there is wise time and space between the compositional touch: heads, hands, torsos, hips, feet moving to the beats of need, now twisting, now bending, resting, conversing, now folding, that diffuse tenderness.

The sequence of physical comportment in cuddling, those poetic constructs of well-rehearsed movements that cajole the needs of one to grow consonant with those of another, resembles choreography. This theater of communicating bodies leaves traces, records, and impressions on bodies and the world. New parents are told the long-term benefits of placing infants on the skin of the rising and falling chest; slavers and jailers make a science of arranging bodies in movement; modern industry (from factories to offices) carefully consider how to manage the intimacies of workers destined to render profit. In this sense, choreography recalls the Greek *khoreia* which means dance and *graphein* which suggests to write/record/describe. The term choreography not only registers the kinesthetic notations of movements in professional dance, it also captures imperceptible corporeal notations of these theatrical movements, giving ways to attend their passing. In writing the futures of bodies in movement, choreography can then also name those often-invisible scripts that direct the actions of individuals much more broadly: the teacher's frown, the social worker's eyebrow, the finger on a trigger. Cuddling as choreography then invites meditation on the kinds of endurances into which this practice is recruited and the subtlety of its effects and affects. If we bear in mind that the actions in a choreography require time to take shape, then it will be no surprise to hear me say that the act of cuddling becomes refined over time. That is to say, cuddling is always historical, embraced by social forces and embracing them.

How could we have been so hopeful as to imagine this intimate archive contained only to the chosen entanglements of loving partners? After all, isn't every cuddle already in the embrace of a world that cuddles the cuddlers? Anyone who has survived the racial embrace, or tried to embrace its survivors, knows that all cuddling is political.

The cuddle connection can activate, even provoke, a breadth of responses. Desire broods in the underlying eroticism of getting someone under your skin. It undermines the beguiling singularity and stability of the self. A fear of abandonment can hide under the cover of comfort and elicit anxious responses: "I got you." Smothering?

A cuddle is an embodied story. We hope that cuddling will be a physical display of "attention, empathetic response, and a commitment to respond to legitimate needs," what Nel Noddings describes as a "caring" practice.[8] We wish for cuddling to be a choreography of care: through the body, with the body, for the body. Until the sixteenth century, the English word care, which comes from the Proto-Germanic word *karō, was used to describe a sense of inward grief, a lamentation. According to the Century Dictionary: "The positive most common senses of care, in English, such as 'to have an inclination' (mid 16th c.); 'to have fondness for' (early 16th c) seem to have developed later as *mirrors* to the earlier negative ones" (emphasis mine). There is a funky echo here of Sigmund Freud's work on the uncanny, and the way he traces how homely and unhomely converge in meaning. Care developed over time through a reflective gesture, a semantic flip. In it, mirror/mirroring as a relational device/action forms/indicates interconnectedness. The relational capacity to reflect and re-orient that belongs to the word care resonates with me, especially in regard to the way I engage with the vibratory and vibration in *On Cuddling*.

But sometimes cuddling is also what Saidiya Hartman calls a scene of subjection. In her work about slavery and its afterlives, Hartman deliberately avoids reading the hyper-visible spectacle of violence against enslaved Black bodies that have been subjected to scrutiny in North American culture, therefore de-sensitizing the public to the pain of Black suffering. Notwithstanding Fred Moten's response to Hartman, on ways that the avoidance is its own invocation, for my purposes,[9] I am interested in how she examines the ordinary and mundane "scenes in which terror can hardly be discerned" to foreground that a violent operational logic is present nonetheless.[10] When systematized, racial violence lurks even when it cannot be perceived, often in practices, policies and policings that name themselves as care.

Of course, many seek reprieve from terror in a cuddle, but for some, cuddling has been terror. In several of the photographs taken by American guards and torturers at Iraq's Abu Ghraib prison and discovered by the media in 2004, the bodies of the incarcerated men are choreographed atop one another, in a coerced cuddlespace. Who was the choreographer? The military and state want to insist it was the sadistic and racist guards, but who or what choreographed them? How did their bodies and minds and imaginations come to embrace such a spectacle, and what forces embraced them that we are told are innocent?

Some of the cuddled are loved to death.[11] Some are suffocated in an embrace. Some, locked in an unchosen hold, improvise, "experiment,"[12] chafe within and against starched uniforms or feel something digging into their back. Others, earlier or later, are given few choices except to cuddle those who will next hold them down—they have to nurse their masters or sooth invaders, often placed in a relation of unpayable debt, as Denise Ferreira da Silva shows us in her reading of Octavia Butler's *Kindred*.[13] Their stories come to bed with us, too. It should not sound melodramatic that I am interested in scenes of subjection that do not appear as choreographies of care and in instances where choreographies of care are emptied out of scenes of subjection. I am likewise concerned with those moments where scenes of subjection are in themselves choreographies of erotics and those where choreographies of erotics empty out scenes of subjection. Care and intimacy have never been foreign to oppression.

We have come to know from Paul Gilroy that slavery is "deeply embedded in modernity."[14] From the history of western modernity, we also know that the world and culture of Blackness at once pose and are posed as a question and an answer. The history of our world—a world where Black people are so often cuddled to death by the state or its agents, a world where Blackness is made to perform itself as cuddly or uncuddly, where black economic activity is both pathologized and exploitable—has been shaped, as Da Silva makes clear, by the global question of how to (mis)manage Black life and the ever-ready answer of Black death. As a question and an answer to the drives of modernity, Blackness's multiple transcriptions on the world are too often cloaked in silence, its contributions function in absence. Homi Bhabha reminds us that the silences and absences come with their own language; he reads the "not-there" "not-moment" times of Blackness; for him, it is "the stressed, dislocatory absence that is crucial for the rememoration of slavery."[15] There is also a stressed, dislocatory absence and silence in the art and discourse of cuddling. There, appearing apparently meaningless in a cuddle is the history of violence a body has endured. There by absence unresolved is a history of Blackness couched in mundane activities devoid of race. Thereby absence.

When envisioned as a scene of subjection or a choreography of care, cuddling can help us map boundaries and thresholds we negotiate but struggle to do so. The geographies of a cuddle offer, to quote Bhabha on borders, "the place from which something begins its presencing."[16] And so, however dead or lively a connection feels in a cuddle, in the charge of two bodies meeting in a heated embrace, attempting to be fluent in each other's histories, journeying in "all directions at once, in all the directions of all the space-times opened by presence to presence,"[17] a cuddle instantiates an ethics of presencing, where tucked-away questions press to find home. To reverse Bhabha's coinage, attention to the cuddle and its histories re-locates the intimate cartography of power and desire. As field and home, cuddling is where new histories are made and embraced. Encoded in the cuddle is a durational till, a temporal causality to bridge a gap in difference.

THE
SLAVE'S FRIEND.

VOL. II, No. II.   WHOLE No. 14.

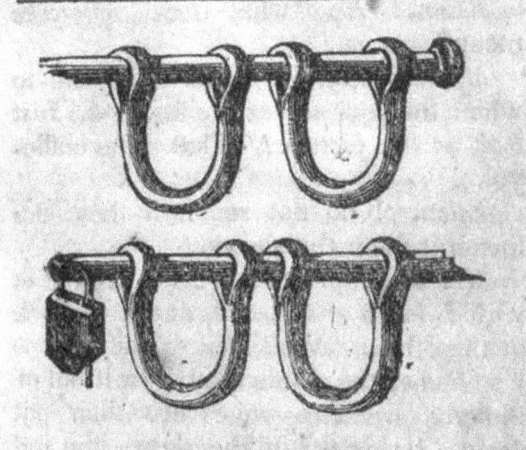

THE COFFLE-YOKE.

Ellen. I never heard the word *coffle* before you took the anti-slavery newspapers, and I do not know exactly what it means. Will you tell me, dear father?

Mr. Murray. I will, my child. Coffle means a number of slaves chained, or hand-cuffed, or yoked together, and dri-

The Slave's Friend, published by the American Anti-Slavery Society, 1837. From the collection of the New York Public Library.

VAG
ABO
NDS

Racial Embrace

In which our author proposes that, drawing on the etymological roots of cuddling, we attend to the way an anti-Black world is built on forms of confinement, captivity, and incarceration that represent the racial embrace.

In opening up the cultural, philosophical, and textual interpretations of cuddling, and in situating the practice of this intimate moment in the racial discourse of Blackness, I wish to queer the seemingly friendly and mundane practice of cuddling by highlighting a set of deadly and generative support structures, in other words a set of "unlimited intimacies."[18] I do so with three aims: (1) to sensitize us to the pain of Black suffering; (2) to ask who benefits from putting countless Black people into a state of social death; (3) to argue, given the global state of anti-Blackness (which makes the search for home so difficult for many Black people), that arc of social death, the social phenomenon sustained through the ideological and repressive structures within a range of social practices and institutions, the phenomenon that Orlando Patterson argues positions Black folks in the US in a "permanent condition of liminality,"[19] is another order of cuddling.

Cuddle, from Old French *coler* meaning "neck, collar," in turn derives from the stem Latin *collare* meaning "necklace, band or chain for the neck." Such connotations connect to the early sixteenth-century use of the word *cull, coll,* meaning "to embrace." This embrace, in the sixteenth century, is linked to *collar,* a word that names the object that encircles a neck indicating bondage (an enslaved) and/or care (a pet) and/or status (a tight necklace, a white- or blue- or pink-collared worker). As a verb, *collar* also implies the act of grasping a body by the neck, or the act of capturing a fugitive.

In tracking the artful and messy movements of the word, in approaching the concept of cuddling more generally, I recall Ann Laura Stoler's reminder that "to study the intimate is not to turn away from structures of dominance but to relocate their conditions of possibility and relations and force of production."[20] The tactile, in addition to what remains unseen, experiences a predicament: her encouragement, in her introduction to *Haunted by Empire*, is to link *intimacy* to its kindred words *intimation* (to hint at or gesture toward) and *intimidation* (to threaten into compliance).

In turning to the etymology of cuddling and intimacy and searching through their lyrical repositories I am seeking to turn our attention to the subtleties that shape the profound vulnerability that conditions what I am calling the "continuous presents" of Black life: the way that, in spite of so many claims to progress and change, anti-Black violence (material, economic, symbolic) recurs and recurs in ways that collapse the familiar temporal categories of past, present and future, just as the past meanings of words shape present-day meanings, imaginations, and future possibilities.

To focus on the racial violence wrapped up in intimacy is not to trivialize it. Examining the thought world of nineteenth-century imperialist liberalism, Lisa Lowe has shown how intimacy is the condition from which capital, empire, and slavery are born. I would add that, by keeping our focus on cuddling, we can learn more about the practices from which this condition emerges. The practice of keeping the neck of enslaved people collared in the yoke, their hands cuffed at the wrists to the coffle chain gets at the fleshy ways of seizing liberty to build empire and make capital. The coffle, as a world-making cuddle technology, for example, marks a poetic origin point for the production of Black vulnerabilities. This technology of confinement and torture then is also an instrument of enforced intimacy. It was in the coffle that diverse African peoples were transformed into objects of servility. It is not only that enslaved Black labor built this world we inherit; the dehumanizing anti-Black system slavery created, depended on, and leaves as its legacy, remains with us today. We are all, in this sense, part of the racial embrace.

But then I am also reminded of the fugitive and maroon sensibilities of cuddling, those fleeing bodies wrapped tightly around one another to hide or for comfort, or those huddled figures waiting in ambush. When refusing the racial embrace, which lays claim to another's futurity, fugitive cuddling lays claims to another futurity.

From this frame of fugitivity I want to bring into focus a kind of cuddling that is organized by the order of states—what I will call *state cuddling*. State cuddling names those practices that attempt to choke fugitivity and the threats it poses to the racial embrace. To understand its violence we must recognize that, to borrow words from Judith Butler, violence "derealizes" life from "established ontolog[ies]": denied a "real" life, their death or suffering becomes unreal.[21] Such a theorization helps us make sense of Black vulnerability as a transnational and postcolonial political crisis. And yet, the racial embrace might signify what becomes reassuring or reaffirming about following the scripts/scores that racial capitalism lays before us, the way identity, understood in this limited sense of vulnerability and anti-Black worldmaking, is seductive, warm, cozy, even if stifling, even for the oppressed sometimes. One can be loved to death in this racial embrace, although it names something both wider and narrower than necropolitics.

On this question of racial embrace, I find myself returning to Sylvia Wynter's argument that the so-called discovery of the Americas in 1492 catalyzed a new European worldview that emerged from fourteenth-century Humanism.[22] Here, one particular "genre" of human based on a European, Christian template was forcibly made into the exemplar of humanity as a whole, with all those non-European genres embraced beneath it as sub- or semi-human, justifying or mandating violence. Later, this hierarchy of the human family, with whiteness at its top, would formalize itself in a scientific discourse of race. While whiteness remains fixed to the top of this genre of the human, the system of this genre decides what other categories to embrace and when and how it embraces these others.

Elsewhere, Wynter makes clear that this European "genre" of "man," which proclaims itself universal, is connected to shifting forms of science, politics, and economics, with devastating impacts. During the Enlightenment, it gave rise to a model, "Man 1," *homo politicus*, that placed non-European others outside the embrace of reason, politics, and legal and moral protection. With the arrival of Darwinism, Man 1 morphed into "Man 2," *homo oeconomicus*, instantiating as the norm the competitive, acquisitive individual, justifying empire and today's forms of racial capitalism as natural or necessary outcomes of human nature.

For Wynter, a strictly economic or political revolution will never be enough: we cannot wrest power from hegemonic forces "without a redescription of the human outside . . . our present descriptive statement of the human, Man, and its over representation."[23] Like many Caribbean thinkers, the tribulations of socialist efforts built on a strict dialectic proved disenchanting; the upheaval in Jamaica during the Manley administration and the afterlives of the Grenada Revolution may well have rejigged how thinkers like Aimé Césaire, Kamau Brathwaite, and Wynter approached dialectic materialism. Wynter offers a redescription of 1492 by reading that moment as "ecosystemic and global systemic 'interrelatedness' of our contemporary situation"[24]: henceforth, we would all be in the shadow of the European notion of "man," ever more so, with no way back, only forward.

We might speak of the genre of man as itself a way of organizing intimacy. Or, to think with critical scholars of infrastructure,[25] we might say that Wynter's work highlights how, under the European genre of the human, intimacy is an infrastructure that facilitates technologies of racialization. These technologies both determine our relations to one another and strive to render Black people as infrastructure to be used for the economic, social, and political "development" of systems of colonialism, imperialism, modernity, and racial capitalism.

Earlier, when I invoked Black vulnerability as a transnational and postcolonial political crisis, the cultural frame I was invoking was "the racist tracts on civilization and history created to justify Western empire," those whose view on African countries, post-independence, was characterized as "afro-pessimism": "the notion that Africa's destiny lies in war, violence, disease, corruption, and hopelessness due to the incapacity of Africans to make improvements in the states of health, poverty, development, peace and governance since the end of the colonial period."[26] While under the sign of the European genre of man, these plagues are imagined as the inevitable expression of Blackness, they in fact reveal the material violence enabled by such imaginative structures in the first place.

If, according to Wynter, we need "new genres of being human," and if under the European genre of man, Blackness is one genre among many uniquely subjugated genres, then Blackness is not a single genre: within other imaginative systems I am embraced by other structures of Blackness.

Wynter teaches us to see Black vulnerability everywhere, so how do we see its slippery traces everywhere in the racial embrace? There is nowhere better to find the productive instability of slipperiness than in the famous United States laws that, for Christina Sharpe, mark "another step in criminalizing black freedom"[27]: the Fugitive Slave Act of 1793 and the similarly named Law of 1850. These Laws not only mandated States to return runaway slaves to their owners, they also allowed Southern slave owners to pursue and retrieve runaway slaves even in free states, to bring along the coffle, that cuddling technology, now given transitive powers by a state eager to keep the peace among whites. The coffle: that instrument of the racial embrace that squeezes fugitivity from a body that is intended to become property.

Recall the escaped bodies huddled together in the tight spaces of refuge. Recall the intimacy between fugitives and those who harbored them. Recall the intimacies of the maroon communities that formed by those that freed themselves. That the Fugitive Slave Act and Law were responses to expand the hold of Southern plantation slavery and to help southern slave owners recover, through capture, "their human property" lost through flight clarifies the work that cuddling does to unsettle the framework of intimacy that conditions capital, empire, and slavery. Marked as "fugitives from justice, and fugitives from slavery,"[28] the legislation that conditions the state of fugitivity resembles cuddling's itinerant choreography, making cuddling, in this state, a crime against property which, as Rinaldo Walcott makes clear, is always already the quintessential crime, and one that Blackness is always threatening to commit.[29]

If the operation of the Fugitive Slave Laws was meant to structure intimacy, then escape is as much a structured intimacy as the laws themselves. We know from the archive of classified advertisements that "many have been obliged to flee precipitately leaving behind them all the little they have acquired since they escaped from slavery."[30] We also know that what you resist persists and stays in the shadows. As a result, to flee precipitately does not subordinate property (the little they have acquired) to escape. Escape is a thing too heavy to carry along with other things. One leaves a place, taking their body, without being noticed. With the guidance of others, they pass out of one existence, laboring into the shadows of another existence, where, as an isolate among other isolates, they sense the charge of their fluid and elusive selves. It is possible to hear in this newspaper report a narrative of communal intimacy. The communal, intimate networked structures of the lives of the fugitive slave, I imagine, informs Amiri Baraka's definition of fugitivity as "that which slides away from the proposed"[31] and helps us understand why Hartman reads Black life in terms of "fugitive gestures of refusal."[32] The sliding gestures of fugitive slaves advance a collective and communal intimacy; such a collective and communal intimacy slides away from the material violence of property and ownership that ties enslaved people in and to place; the intimacy proposed incites a practice that says *you cannot hold me down*. The fugitive slave, at once, incites a culture of intimacy and resistance. It is this intimacy of resistance that rejects the intimacy of the European genre of man.

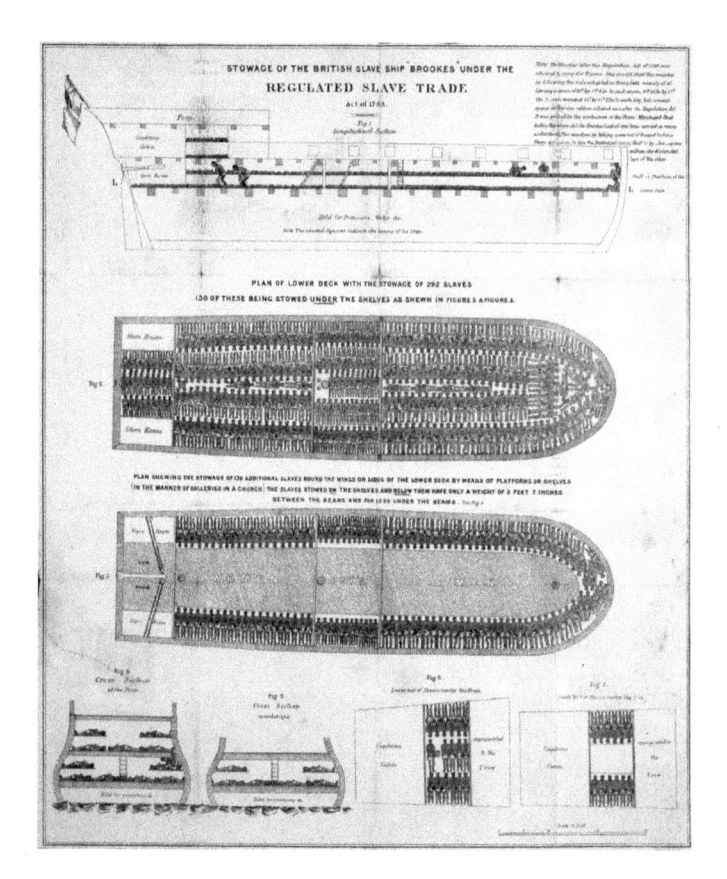

Stowage of the British slave ship "Brookes" under the Regulated Slave Trade Act of 1788, c. 1788. From the collection of the Library of Congress.

Hold. Womb. Tomb. Spoon.

In which the author asks us to consider how Black bodies were made to cuddle through the paradigmatic and world-making technology of the slave ship, which transmuted them into commodities, and so entreats us to consider the violent and intimate origins of our markets, but also asks us to dwell with the forms of creativity and community that then emerges into the world.

Hold as an act of gripping; hold as a space of enclosure[33]—in other words, a structure to support storage.[34] Hold as a messy thesis for intimacy.

In this chapter I will explore the racial embrace through two images. First, the diagram of the slave ship *Brookes* that was so fatefully distributed by abolitionists in Britain starting in 1788, which depicts impossible but revealing cross-sections and cutaway views of the vessels and the horrific, tight conditions of the upwards of 600 African people stowed in its hold. Adam Hochschild writes well of the historical importance of the *Brookes* diagram as the first piece of modern advertising and the first piece of social movement propaganda.[35]

Second, I turn to an anti-abortion billboard campaign that appeared in New York and other US cities depicting a cute young Black girl and the slogan "the most dangerous place for an African

American is in the womb." Dorothy Roberts' work teaches us to read this billboard within a genealogy of racist eugenics movements that reframed Black people and particularly Black women as a genetic threat to the white body politic, even to themselves and their loved ones.[36]

I will read the billboard and the *Brookes* diagram as advertisements. Today, advertising is so ubiquitous that this descriptor has little resonance. But I want to dwell with advertising as a form of visual messaging that, in Walter Benjamin's sociopsychological approach to modernity, appears as the emanation of a far-from-innocent dreamworld. Through advertising, an image becomes "the ruse by which the dream forces itself on industry."[37] In this sense, both images can be seen as rhetorical artefacts, intended to convince but also to habituate the imagination. They raise questions of the violence of representation and the violence enacted on the viewer.

In *The Arming and Fitting of English Ships of War, 1600–1815*, Brian Lavery describes how "The hold was designed to stow items in bulk, where the inaccessibility of an individual cask did not matter. Other stores had to be kept in storerooms, on racks, on shelves, and in drawers, where they could be reached very quickly in an emergency."[38] This design history of the hold depicts an enclosure designed for both care and neglect (not mattering).

Here, then, in the intimate social space of the hold, where "strangers" found themselves "in anomalous intimacy,"[39] holding was not simply a metaphor to soften the uses of the slave ship.

In the archives of maritime worlds, the slave ship was a paradigmatic technology of modernity and one that inspired many other institutions: a machine that was simultaneously a prison, a factory, a market, and a maritime instrument of warfare.[40] It indexes legal and social relations that inaugurated the economic, discursive, and institutional life of transnational capitalism. (The double use of the word 'store.' We care for our stores of value.) The hold, a carceral/imperial/industrial cuddlespace, was a laboratory for the biopolitical regulation of intimacies that structure Black life, then and today, particularly the reproductive capacities of Black women, their womb, and their maternal and affective labor.

If Black women's wombs were capitalized in the brutal economic system that designed the hold (for cuddling limbs) as a capital generating nucleus then we must invite ourselves to meditate on the various scales of cuddling that coexisted in the chambers of these dungeons. Here, the funky disenchantment of the unconsoled still roam the stenching air that beholds the hollow chest of the hold. Here, Wilson Harris argues, limbo was born, as purgatory and as dance. Harris configures the grooves on the hold as a "limbo gateway" into cross-cultural community. For him, the limbo also fosters a "new corpus of sensibility" "an inter-tribal or cross-cultural community of families"[41] and from the vestige of blood, dirt, piss, shit, and sweat. I imagine a hand voluntarily reaching for (home) another hand, in-between not caring so much if it concludes its mission and willing a form forward; I imagine the longing hand reaching, alivening metals that hold other limbs in place into a recording technology that captures percussions the body recalls. Call this reach Praise, assessing sounds of the past. Praise = Portal. This portal is not to wheel out captive percussion, those made now by metals on limbs exposed to elements; more so to open cells onto a then there for someone now here to listen in on. I am not so naive as to empty out the vast terror in percussion. Terror is percussive in correspondence. And yet, reaching *for* reaches *back*, too; it is recursive. It passes back through the heart to another place where laughter not blood gushes into walls that mind the scratchings of those who offered themselves for others to arrive. Here, unarrivants line and dot flimsy floors that forensics will swim their noses and guts through; here, I imagine no sorcery nor sword, only willful hands reaching, levitating this confine, re-configuring the pitch the Atlantic makes to turn stomachs and bang bodies into bodies.

Call all this alchemy creation; call this creation ungenesis. Not of Adams, not of Eves. Of a world that reaches back. This world beckons me now and I am beckoning you so, who knows, even if you cannot hear, listen for it: there is value in muscling for a reach, there is shape to the sound reaching makes. Call it a hymn, a hand humming the distance. Call this evidence of cargo rebellion. Call it not not mattering.

The *Brookes* was the first popular image of a slave ship published by the Plymouth chapter of the Society for Effecting the Abolition of the Slave Trade, based on information provided by William

Elford. This drawing was widely featured in abolitionist propaganda, and the ship was indelibly
associated in the European and American imagination with the slave trade. Built in 1781 and
named after Liverpool slave trading merchant
Joseph Brookes Jr., who commissioned it and
was its first owner, *Brookes* was referred to as "a
capital ship" because of its many voyages.[42] The
London Abolitionist committee, which apparently
approved the Plymouth broadside, thought it necessary, in leading organizer Thomas Clarkson's
words, "to select some one ship, which had been
engaged in the Slave-trade, with her real dimensions, if they meant to make a fair representation
of the manner of the transportation."[43] Clarkson explained in his history of the abolitionist
movement that the image made "an instanta-
neous impression of horror upon all who saw it."
He points out it gave viewers "a much better idea
than they could otherwise have had of the horrors
of [the Africans'] transportation and contributed
greatly . . . to impress the public in favour of our
cause."[44]

Let us look closely at the caricatured bodies of
the enslaved people that, for Spillers, look "like so
many cartoon figures."[45] Is it not a scene of cuddling? This image offers us a way to think about
those "monstrous intimacies" to which Sharpe
draws our attention in her book titled with the
same moniker and by which she encourages us
to consider "those subjectivities constituted from
transatlantic slavery onward and connected, then
as now, by the everyday mundane horrors that

aren't acknowledged to be horrors."[46] Cuddling, for some, is an everyday horror.

In the autobiographical *The Interesting Narrative of the Life of Olaudah Equiano*, first published in 1789, we learn that "the [slave] ship's cargo were confined together" and that "the stench of the hold . . . was so intolerably loathsome [that] it became absolutely pestilential." Here, in the hold, Equiano acknowledges smell as part of the everyday mundane horrors that the ship's cargo had to live with. "The closeness of the place, and the heat of the climate, added to the number in the ship, which was so crowded that each had scarcely room to turn himself, almost suffocated us." He doesn't spare us "the shrieks of the women, and the groans of the dying." These, together, he tells us, "rendered the whole scene of horror almost inconceivable."[47] That the degree of horror was *almost* inconceivable in this scene of cuddling (narrated through the senses of horror—touch, smell, and sound) provides a portal for understanding the ways enslaved folks resisted the cuddle of slavery; this adverb primes us to inquire into the imaginative and physical states of habitations in the hold that made the horror generated by these pestilential intimacies very nearly not horrible.

The publication of the bestselling *Interesting Narrative* coincided with Thomas Clarkson's *Essay on the Slave Trade*, based on an interview with a sailor who worked on a slave ship. The sailor reported that "the misery which the slaves endure in consequence of too close a stowage is not easy to describe." In 1790, responding to the publicized horrors of slavery, a British House of Commons committee interviewed Dr. Thomas Trotter, a physician working on *Brookes*, about the conditions of enslaved people on the slave-ship. Asked whether the "slaves had room to turn themselves," Trotter replied:

> No. The slaves that are out of irons are locked "spoonways" and locked to one another. It is the duty of the first mate to see them stowed in this manner every morning; those which do not get quickly into their places are compelled by the cat [a whip] and, such was the situation when stowed in this manner, and when the ship had much motion at sea, they were often miserably bruised against the deck or against each other. I have seen their breasts heaving and observed them draw their breath, with all those laborious and anxious efforts for life which we observe in expiring animals subjected by experiment to bad air of various kinds.[48]

If we conjoin the sailor's language of bruising misery to Equiano's language of closeness and confinement and bring them to bear on Trotter's reply then we notice that abolitionists staged the management of Black bodies on slave ships through the language of cuddling (spoonways). Cocooned in violence, here, as well as in *Brookes*, which Simone Browne reads the *Brooks* diagram to highlight ways that "the tiny black figures are made to seem androgynous, interchangeable, and replicable."[49] Cocooned in violence, their unchosen proximities reveal the conditions wherein new forms of togetherness were necessarily constituted. Browne notes that the seemingly emotional characteristics of the tiny Black figures challenge perception "with a closer look." "One can see that each of the tiny black figures are not replicas of each other; rather, some have variously crossed arms, different gestures, or seem to turn to face one another, while some stare and look back at the gaze from nowhere."[50] Such contorted togetherness, such fugitive solidarity defined Black life at an origin on the middle passage and still does today.

In Édouard Glissant's *Poetics of Relation* he describes "the boat" (the slave ship) as "a womb, a womb abyss."[51] If we take the womb space as a cuddlespace, what would it mean to understand it as "a place of encounter and connivance"?[52] While for Glissant this place of making is the sea, the abyss in cuddling opens up a place of encounter and connivance. How can this place of insidious subjection also be a place from which one shapes power and build relations and protests monstrous intimacies? For Glissant, "the belly of this boat dissolves" victims of the slave trade and, at the same time, "precipitates them into a non-world from which [they] cry out." To emphasize this terrifying reality, Glissant argues, "This boat [,] pregnant with as many dead as living under sentence of death[,] . . . generates the clamour of [enslaved peoples'] protests."[53]

Glissant's gendered metaphor of the slave ship as a womb brings home Ruth Miller's argument for the womb as a material space around which political decisions take place.[54] As a reproductive technology that reproduces Black labor power, the ship-as-womb foregrounds the intersection between reproduction and biopolitics and helps us to think of ways Black wombs were made into a forge of enslavement. Schoolteacher, the sinister and abusive slaver and race scientist in Toni Morrison's *Beloved*, echoes the reality, confirmed by historians, that slave masters valued enslaved pregnant bodies because they viewed the unborn babies as a future source of labor or new property to sell.[55] Yet these infants were also destined for death. Hartman reminds us that the womb "bore an uncanny resemblance to the grave, making plain the fact that the living eventually would assume their station among the ranks of the dead."[56] The temporal modification in Hartman's eventually does not protect us from the simultaneity of life and death. The site of life is also a death sentence, a grave site, a womb-tomb. What is the philosophy of relation between the womb/ hold and the cuddling womb and cuddling hold? I am happy that the womb-tomb reappears in Glissant's *Philosophie de la Relation*, the last text we know of his, where he specifically engages it in relation to his own mother.[57] I say happy because it demands us to dwell with the cuddling Black womb, along with the "[b]lood and shit" that Hartman, speaking about the hold, says "ushered us into the world,"[58] insisting we think about the womb in the Black body, and not simply the scene of surveillance and regulation in the cuddling hold. Doing so not only doubles the long history of capital accumulation of the hold, it reveals the ways that such accumulation is contiguous with the infringements on Black people's reproductive health and rights.

In February 2011, a three-story-high billboard appeared in the recently gentrified SoHo neighborhood of New York City featuring an adorable little Black girl in a pink dress and a slogan proclaiming "The Most Dangerous Place for an African American Is in the Womb." The year before, in Atlanta, a similar billboard appeared with a little Black boy and the inscription "Black Children Are an Endangered Species." The advertising campaign was funded by Life Always, a Texas evangelical anti-abortion group and was clearly calculated to prey on both Black parents' fears as well as a certain form of paternalistic white benevolence. Drawing on Hortense Spillers' work, Sharon Holland argues that Black women's bodies have become a crucial symbolic space between life and death.[59] Life Always' social choreography, with its tactically shocking images that present themselves as advocating the protection of Black children but they mark an everyday scene of "subjection in which we are all forced to participate."[60] The billboard, then, leans into how "racial slavery," as Jennifer Morgan points out, "functioned euphemistically as a social condition forged in African women's wombs."[61] The billboard leans into this social condition and naturalizes the womb of the Black gestating body as a tomb. Hence, to be birthed by her is to be assumed to live a bad life; her appearance in the public imagination jeopardizes the possibility of a good life for good citizens. In this way, the billboard operates euphemistically; given the disregard for Black life in North America, the campaign's saccharine claims to care for the welfare of Black children is a decoy. Instead, it functions to reify Black wombs as inhospitable, and participate in controlling Black reproductive freedom and the freedom of the lives that it makes possible.

The billboard's effectiveness stems in part from the way it refracts the conventional imaginaries that haunt the global Black world, for instance in cartoonish representations where the Western bulge of Africa, as depicted in most maps, is refigured as a swollen Black woman's belly, pregnant with the hungry, typically as a warning about "overpopulation" and the need to, again, control Black reproduction. What does a formulation of the pregnant Black body cuddling the fetus do in relation to medical discourse of "risk" around pregnancy that construct racialized and poor wombs as (potentially, probably) inhospitable environments for the fetus and threats to planetary well-being, therefore in need of management, surveillance, and correction? I recall Sharon Holland's argument about the ongoing ways in which Black subjects "share the space the dead inhabit."[62] Here, we are called to account for how Black people are cast as what Abdul JanMohamed calls "the death bound subjects."[63]

And yet, what do we make of the value assigned to the Black womb as an engine of cuddling? As an important site of capital regeneration and accumulation, scientific inquiry, and moral discourse?

Still.

The Black womb is also something else for the Black womb-owner-and-issue. As much as it is an object of abuse, subject of and to material and discursive terrors, it is as well a site of joy, and speculation, and futurity. Given what we know about pregnancy, it is also a site that yields ambivalence and anxiety, especially given the shocking statistics in the US and elsewhere that indicate that systemic racism drastically increases maternal health risks for Black adults and infants.[64]

Yet the womb is not the only site and symbol of the reproductive labor assigned to Black women within racial capitalism. One simply needs to think about the popular pancake mix brand, Aunt Jemina, which uses the nineteenth-century mammy figure to advertise a product it proclaims to save labor, to see how undeniable Black maternal labor is foundational to the economics and social exchange within American (popular) culture. The personification of hospitality (service economy) through the servitude of the Black cook conflates the technologies of the kitchen with those of race and gender. Technologies in the sense of how it interpolates Black women as particular kinds of subjects, whose domestic labor tends to be outside the frame at the same time that that labor tends to hold together everything in the frame of the social body. As Sharpe notes, "the terror of that 'kitchen space' will be unremembered and come over to be figured as a privileged space of blackness because of a spatial, and also perhaps visual proximity to whiteness."[65]

In contending with the cuddle womb and the cuddle hold, how do we cuddle death? I bring us back to the slave ship. In sailor speak, spooning is a maneuvering technique. According to a 1708 *Sea*

Dictionary, spooning refers to means of putting a ship directly "before wind and sea waves, without the assistance of a sail. A sailor typically decides to spoon when, in a great storm, a ship is so weak with age or from laboring that a sailor dare not lay her under the sea. Sometimes, to make the ship go steadier, they set the foresail, and the ship is placed in a spooning position."[66] In this way, spooning happens in the absence of the spoon-like shape of the sails (its concave form), suggesting the propelling ability of (water) spooning.

For a sailor to spoon a ship, they must be sure there is sea room, enough room for them to maneuver the ship safely, without encountering hazards.[67] And yet, as Equiano and the physician Dr. Thomas Trotter points out, there is very little room, no sea room, for the enslaved in the hold. This closely packed room, according to *The Sailor's Word-Book*, is called Spoon-ways: "In slave-ships, stowing the poor wretches so closely locked together, that it is difficult to move without treading upon them"[68] In this context, I wonder what in the hold makes spooning seem like an excellent sleeping position, a relaxing way to sleep? In sailing, to move rapidly on or upon another vessel is another way sailors understand spooning. When I say this fleshy intimacy is fundamental to the project of modernity, it is not lost on me how the shape of one sought after commodity (literal spoons)[69] forms the basis of the design that shapes the space that another sought after commodity (bodies). As a multi-functional symbol, this everyday utensil, useful for eating, measuring, cooking and serving, has navigational and political significance.

Writing about the social life of those shipped, Fred Moten and Stefano Harney position hapticality as a condition/gift/terror for enslaved people: enlivening possibilities exist in this confined closeness. Enslaved folks teach us "the capacity to feel through others, for others to feel through you, for you to feel them feeling you" in ways that are "not regulated, at least not successfully, by a state, a religion, a people, an empire."[70] To make a way from all that spooning. Another new language, this spoonway, a new foreign language, this sailor speak, pumping against each compressing (a language in a press of another language). Serving spoons.

The Irwin Clement Caribbean steel band, Stalbridge Street, Maryle-
bone, London, 1963. Photo Henry Grant, via the Museum of
London/Heritage Images/Getty Images.

The Dead Can Love Us Too

After Jimmy Robert's *Untitled (Fragments)*

Jigsaw of leaves of my brother's head howl
delivering a puzzle into cavities on-the-block.
Jigsaw of leaves now my brother's head howl
all day delivering a puzzle made this blood
into cavities on the block's ear.
Jigsaw of leaves and my brother's head howl
a puzzle made to scatter into cavities.

Jigsaw of leaves now my brother's head howls
a jigsaw leaves my brother's head
cavities on the block's ear.
Jigsaw leaves my brother's head suddenly howling
a jigsaw of leaves now my brother's head
morphing a puzzle of blood into cavities
on the block's ear.

Jigsaw of leaves of my brother's head howls
jigsaws of leaves of others' brothers
scattering a puzzle suddenly blood morphing
a puzzle now love into cavities. On the block
breath reverses willed returns
the ins and outs of jigsaw injustice
a tide that still carves pleasure into the face
who faces terror.

A jigsaw howls my brother's head leaves
a black tide who carves pleasure at the face of
terror

> a jigsaw leaves my brother's head
> not scattering blood
> a puzzle refusing coffin refusing to be block
> the self from self of injustice
> all I am not I am also
> a jigsaw of leaves of my brother's head
> puzzling the video from a covered camera,
> the Velcro
> straps put over badges.
> Jigsaw of leaves of my brother's head howls
> hammering down houses that carve pleasure out
> the face of terror, a jigsaw of leaves of my
> brother's head
> scatter a puzzle made of blood morphosizing all
> I am not also

the dead: even as I must die howling I am saying
I love you.
dead: even if I must die howling into cavities on
the block hear me say I love you.
dead: even if I must die howling it into cavities
on the block I am saying I love you.
dead: even if I must die I am saying I love you.
dead: I am saying I love you even if I must howl
into cavities on the bloc.

> My brother's head
> on the block
> 's ear drums the staccato of gunfire of an
> invading army.

On Cuddling

Phanuel Antwi

My brother's mouth,
lipped sealed, is a rebel's testimony nosing
around, following procedure: bottom-up shirt
neat cuts a tie.
My brother's unrests,
not as they exist but as I see them, shed a
thread of light through heads. Hair lines up to
testify, while eyes, chinned up, croon to the sky,
testifyin' that part as itself is myth is a mirror, an
I knotting I, shattering across, untying necks on
the block.

I breathe breathe I breathe I I breathe I: declare
your breath. That willed return is breath
reversing shards of my brother's head into the
block's ear.

suddenly breath, this equalizer of beats, guts in
its precision.
your "suddenly" has been [howling] always.
(suddenly growing redundant weighs)
even if my always is now your suddenly / even
if my always is yours now hear me say I am less
the speaker of this poem than
the person loving the subjects
of the poem
even if my always
is now your suddenly
even if my always
is your suddenly

now hear me howling into cavities

even if we must die
on the block say
who are these men
who take my time
for granted.

Grammars of the
Black Atlantic

In which our author dares us to recognize the coerced and also the queer intimacies convoked in the hold of the slave ship and the way these continue to hold us in, or hold us to, or hold us with, or hold us from certain coercive forms of cuddling in the continuous present.

Stories that give accounts of the sexual violence enslaved people endured on slave ships are well-known. We know little, however, about the intimacies enslaved people enjoyed among themselves in their gender-segregated holds. If I attend to the lives and existence of enslaved ancestors, then I also believe that the enslaved men and women lived for themselves in the holds of the slave ships, they were not extensions of the enslavers' integrity. In other words, the intimacy developed as a result of bodies having to lay very close to one another in the hold of *Brookes* in order for capital to accumulate is not the only story. I believed that the architecture of the hold ushered the bodies of these people to enter a place of encounter and connivance and, in this space of stretched surprise, cuddling opens up new grammar for relations in the hold. This new relational grammar that might have emerged from the coercive gendered horrors underpinning the slave system haunts us to this day. The form of the hold shape what is made real in its confines: the grand economic territory of capital, which is also a mobile coffin: The Black Atlantic bequeathed to Black people and all people in the US and the world. In tracing the contours of the hold, I have in mind to understand the origins of what Gargi Bhattacharyya calls "cuddly capitalism,"[71] those forms of contemporary capitalism that afford some the illusion of peace, justice, dignity, and care, while necessarily denying it to others, near and far.

And yet, the violent accounting for how to construct the hold—this space of coerced intimacy that is genuine and sustaining and dangerous and constricting—did not always constrict how the people held in there lived. Along with Audre Lorde, I know "that part of the understanding process is grammatical." Lorde taught us that grammar "served a purpose, that it helped to form the way we thought, that it could be freeing as well as restrictive." Grammar, of the restrictive hold of the ship, operates with a biocapital sensibility: does Lorde, in conversation with Adrienne Rich, not remind us that, "tenses are a way of ordering the chaos around time"?[72] This stress on time scales questions around symbolic freedom under enslavement, making me believe that the new relational grammar, in a hold, is a beacon of freedom.

When I began this project, I went looking for evidence of this grammar to legitimize my sense that queer acts happened on the ship. I was after traces that might liven up the sentient archives of the lives lived in the hold. I was aware of Jose Esteban Munoz's teaching on the ephemerality of evidence, particularly those involving queer acts.[73] But my inability to verify them nagged me to seek after the legitimacy of colonial documents (travel narratives) and from fields (anthropology and history) as a way to make visible the archives I believed to be there by their absence. I learned about the presence of lesbian practices in Africa in the form of female-husbands through the case study of Queen Njinga Mbanda, who ruled over the Ndongo Kingdom (present day Angola) in 1624 and who led a four-decade military resistance effort against Portuguese dominion. These helped me understand what Hortense Spillers means when she argues that, under patriarchal society, the system and legacy of slavery thrived, and that "the customary lexis of sexuality" and gender were thrown "into unrelieved crisis."[74] I hear her to mean that slavery threw African's gender and sexuality matrix into crisis and also that, in the afterlife of slavery, hegemonic gender/sexuality for everyone is in "unrelieved crisis," haunted by the legacy of slavery. The constellation of this crisis destabilizes the unnoticed rules of gender and sexuality, estranging the continuous present. That is to say, there's a disruption in the customary journey from the past to the present. My turn to cuddling, you can say, is then a way to disrupt the epistemological dread, the way the world places Blackness in a suffocating embrace, that shapes and orders our imagination, including sexuality.

In her 1974 essay "The Politics of Intimacy" Spillers instructs us to "perceive the 'politics of intimacy' as a dialectical encounter, rather than an antagonism of opposites; in other words, the situation requires conversation, the act of living among others, in all the dignity and concentration that the term implies. It is this tension in our dynamic experience which shocks our mythic expectations."[75] The dynamic experience of enslaved folks living among enslaved others, and in the collectivity of such others, means that enslaved people in the hold practiced their own counter-holding; however, the archive of those counterholds have been erased; and this because they represented some kind of threat to the pro-to-state-cuddling of the slave ship and its world (the anvil on which our world was tempered). And yet, its legacy continues in the funky counterholding of queer/trans Black people.

In the confines of the hold, the grammars of queer intimacy appear to instantiate different world-making processes. We know from deconstructionists that the making of a universalizing meaning is a matter of tying down conventions and holding them in place. The work I've been doing so far in *On Cuddling*, has been to think with the conventional choreography of cuddling but untie its contractual institutions—its grammatological adherence to comfort and romance—as a way to transform the all too often dualistic and subordinating attitude that guides the mis/management of Black lives. Playing with the sign and structure of cuddling, then, is an attempt to disclose the crevices in which complex intimacies lie unnamed; in the nexus of estrangement made possible by playing, grammar holds traces of instituted intimacies. If a function of grammar is to structure the everyday experience of communicating humans, and if we do not tether grammar to sentences (language) and allow ourselves to consider ways the laws that govern sentences of the nation-state in turns choreograph Black death sentences, then we might start to reconsider how the structuralist approach to grammar, an approach that would have us distinguish and separate subject from object, noun from verb, would foreclose the disorienting disruption of Black life to grammars of everyday life.

What I mean to say is that grammar is part of the phenomenon of the cuddly capitalist confine, rather than external to what it observes. Grammar, then, is not a measurement; it marks an interaction. In this sense, cuddling foregrounds a grammar of interaction, one in which part of a limb makes itself known to another part. In the universe of the cuddlespace, one part of the universe makes itself intelligible to another part of the universe in its ongoing differentiating intelligibility and materialization. In this way, cuddlers and other poets do not measure time; they maneuver around, even spoon time; they create time through changing, changing together. What is the nature of change if it is not cause and effect, if there is no trajectory? (No "progress"? No teleology?) What can we then shed of grammar, given its very logic is built on assumptions born of the hold? We cannot say everything at once. But that is what it is to experience history, no? In any moment, to feel history all at once? Time has a history = the entirety of the history is what is still happening. Cuddling's grammar of inter-action shows how grammar struggles to yield to entanglements.

Within the anti-totalizing context of the Black Atlantic, where entanglement does not resolve into easy unions, Spillers turns our attention toward the symbolic order instantiated by another euphemism: She writes of the African slave trade in the US as "an American grammar." For her this grammar remains grounded in the originating metaphors of captivity and mutilation so that it is as if neither time nor history (nor historiography and its topics) show movement, as if the human subject is "murdered" over and over again in the continuous present. Which is to say, for her, the journey of the Middle Passage and the holds in which Black bodies were packed like animals con-stitute what she calls the "American grammar." This is her way of saying that the materiality of the body is equally marked by the violent power in language and grammar to obfuscate, conceal, and abdicate responsibility in the history of slavery. I have turned to cuddling to access a grammar of queer intimacy because I relish the funk in a cud-dle's journey, and because the social and intimate grammars of queer intimacies in the Black Atlan-tic were not always recorded. We need to shimmer the stories out of the record, inventing, reinvent-ing, organizing, reorganizing, agonizing, and recognizing, these are all part of readying our-selves to behold the textual ghosts of bodies in the archives.

Shimmering the archive is a funky move. That funk accumulates. Accrual is a prevailing archival grammar in the Black Atlantic, and so we must heed Stephanie Smallwood's instructions: we must account for the "counterfactual" as a way to give "interpretive weight"[76] to the internal experience of the enslaved; the counterfactual shimmers into archival abundance, marking an impossibility for completion and a potential for alterations. How can it not? Black intimacies in the hold of the ship are monstrous and shimmering. Queer intimacies in the Black Atlantic gesture toward something monstrous and shimmering. To go searching for Black queer intimacies in the Black Atlantic is to course through boundless monstrous shimmerings. Stumbling and fumbling and bumping are joys of the course. Searching them, by ways of experiencing others clutching scars to clutch on life, makes cuddling's historiography in the Black Atlantic necessarily poetic.

I turn to the joys in the poetic Black Atlantic because historiography on queerness tends to index an engrossing agony: the invisibility or silence of queer social life constitutive of official archives. This index has taught scholars of queer archives to read along and against empiricist research methods that privilege the visual or readily available documents. This expands the research sensorium. Queer evidence is not always on display, nor is it given the space to flaunt itself in the archive. To borrow from Dionne Brand, queer evidence exists as "a prism, distorted and shimmering . . . [:] appearing and disappearing. An absence presence. Though few of us have seen it, or consciously attach importance to it,"[77] we know to prepare ourselves for the unexpected.

We prepare for experiences of unexpectedness because we know from Muñoz that we have to attend to "fleeting moments" and "performances" because they "evaporate at the touch of those who would eliminate queer possibility";[78] and we also prepare so our bodies can be ready for unexpected pleasures in the archives' choreography. While the shimmering and the fleetingness lean us toward the ephemeral and the opaque, this also reminds us of the perils of leaving too much evidence. By the grace of sweat, I have come to understand queer intimacy through the frame of marronage, thanks to the work of Jarrett Brown and Ronald Cummings.[79] Their work moves queer historiography from its oppositional character of normativity-anti-normativity, and visibility-invisibility, dyads that overlook life's simultaneous comings and goings. Their work asks us to think of maroon practices as practices of queer intimacy and to attend to shimmering moments in the archive.

What forms of social life and opportunities for disidentification from our Manichaean fantasies can we escape when we center queerness in trans-atlantic slavery studies and orient toward different evidentiary possibilities? We can turn to the inti-mate matters of slavery, which, in turn, turns us to the dangerous duties of care born out of complex intra African relations of power on the slave ships that transported Africans into the Americas. Such a turn requires that we abandon "an obsession with a single origin" and "pure original values" associated with the people who lived such lives; letting go of the obsession might allow access to the "unprecedented potential for contact" that took place on and before arriving on the ship; this kind of detour is, for Glissant, "a return to the point of entanglement, from which we were forcefully turned away."[80]

To turn toward this point of entanglement reveals intimate bonds not organized around reproductive futurity or heteronormative patriarchy as its site of world remaking. Omise'eke Natasha Tinsley's "Black Atlantic, Queer Atlantic" shows us how. She traces the etymology of the Suriname word mati, which translates as "my girl," but has its roots in the word for shipmate. As in: "she who served the Middle Passage with me."[81] Ship mate intimacies were "how queer relationships were forged on merchant and pirate ships, where Europeans and Africans slept with fellow—and I mean same-sex—sailors. And, more powerfully and silently, how queer relationships emerged in the holds of slave ships that crossed between West Africa and the Caribbean archipelago." This is what, according to Tinsley, "Paul Gilroy never told us" about the Black Atlantic.[82] She goes on to argue that "captive African women created erotic bonds with other women in the sex-segregated holds, and captive African men created bonds with other men. In so doing, they resisted not-mattering and the commodification of their bought and sold bodies by *feeling* and *feeling for* their co-occupants on these ships."[83] The queer Black Atlantic navigates these crosscurrents as it enfolds enslaved and African, brutality and desire, genocide and resistance. Here, fluidity is not an easy metaphor for queer and racially hybrid identities but for concrete, painful, *and* liberatory experience. Through the *ands*, we search for ways to account for the orgasms and pleasures of these bonds.

And yet, I still wonder, how do we imagine intimacy and erotics outside the fold of our habituated feeling for agency? Do subjects without agency embody erotics? Embody desire? How do we unbind the bond between agency and desire that tethers subjectivity in the shadow of what Wynter calls "Man"? Do we need to? How important are these questions when the archives under consideration do not concern the making of the subjects I am searching for? Given this artifact is not African, how does what we see challenge what is represented?

If seeing as a sensory experience does not eviscerate how this sensory information interfaces our body to the world, then the relational tactility of cuddling, and its investment in destabilizing a hierarchy of senses, gestures to how, as sensory beings, we know through sensory overlap. LaMonda Horton Stallings understands the multifold form of the senses as a multisensory philosophy; she calls it funk and sits this philosophy within a tradition of improvisation. In *Funk the Erotics: Transaesthetics and Black Sexual Cultures* she attends to the many ways to behold the reconnective sensory work of funk: of how the sensory (sound, smell, and taste), embodied movement (dance and sex), and force (mood and will), offer a method to do the work of intimacy, sexuality, labor, and Black cultural production. I am moved by Stallings' attention to how sexual cultures "translate, produce and

reproduce Black pleasure, pain, intimacy, relationality, individuality, and communality in the face of
historical and ever-changing sexual terror and violence."[84] I am particularly moved by how it has
me searching for the rebellious investment in the
bodies of those who lived the funk of the hold and
my corporeal desires to imagine the potential full
lives lived in the funk of the hold. And this search
must include, as Treva B. Lindsey and Jessica
Marie Johnson demonstrate "the erotic mapping
of slavery and resistance."[85] Tinsley, Stallings, and
Lindsey and Johnson offer a capacious embrace
of juxtapositions.

Limbo, for example, is typically seen as a trivial
dance craze. But the practice originates in a dance
in which enslaved people sneaked their weight
into themselves, suspended themselves from the
constraints of living under deck, by folding their
bodies into communion with itself. Imprinted in
the folds is a "new corpus of sensibility,"[86] one that
embraces bodily appetites, the body's pain and
pleasures, as a possible way to convey one's accep-
tance, appeal and rejection of their lot. The utility
in this state of limbo, of bones folding on bones
to hold one still, from the ground, storing sweet
bitter memories in between bones, reassembles
and finds release in the flexes and slow staccato
progressions of popping and locking, styles inher-
ited by Hip Hop culture that funk dancers know
too, too well.

My interest in this long arm of funk and its
sweaty sensuality is in its ability to conjure physical interactions across historical moments at the
same time that it holds deep expressions of histor-

ical knowledge in and out of sync, in and out of shared time and space. Much like the choreography of cuddling.

The close sociality of the slave ship's hold and the dance floor is not mere conjecture nor a profane act, desecrating a sacred space. We notice cuddling's constant doubleness at Fort Good Hope at Senya Beraku, in Ghana, where slave castles and dungeons that once held captured Africans before they crossed the shores of Africa to be enslaved into Blackness in the Americas now function as storage for all sorts of holdings: from crates of beer for the parties that take place at the courtyards of these castles to the accouterments of rest-house businesses, from televisions to children's bikes. Whether these shifts are improvising or reclaiming the meaning of the physical space, we cannot overlook the reinvention: of locals "us[ing] the forts as they wish."[87]

There is a moment in Dionne Brand's visionary novel *What We All Long For* that I tended to skip over because it confounded my understanding. I now know the improvisational capacities of funk tends to confound. Mobilizing the multisensory field of funk, Brand frames the beginning of Chapter 7 with a list of Black music icons in the visual voice of hip-hop rhymes and takes on the design of a musical advertisement. We encounter the funk in the inventory, attend to the multi consciousness on the page, and, in the discrete discipline used to organize history and expose/ establish historical relations of musical traditions on the page, see-hear the sympathetic tones and resonances between sound expressions. We enjoy how DJs in DJ cultures use the resonances and tones of these histories to remake the world funky and, moreover, as we sit with the diverse dynamic views of Black sounds that the list displays, imagine the smell of dancers in the cuddle of a dance floor, deep in the funky grammar of sweat, exchanging bodily muck.

Quadraphonic, Jo Jo Flores, Paul E. Lopez, Boris Kid Conga, Divine Earth Essence, Live percussion by Tribalism's, Saturday 18. Oz/ Off Centre PJ Patric Forge, Movement, Lond., U.K., Da late, computer of rebirth of Cool., Aku John Kong, OJ Palma at Roxy Blu, Confusion, Design/vice, Soul Power, DJ spin, with resident DJs Semis & Kila, Una has! Ziolay 21st disco, hip-hop house, soul-funked/Brazilian/OJ John Laumahara, Fiction Design Co.'s men's and women's summer collection. Exclusive up roc/FDCO 416 Fashion, Juice/solid Garage featuring Jephte Guillarme—New York—born in Haiti, uprooted to Brooklyn with his family, turning vodun spirituality into something understood. Hit single "The Prayer." Voyage Dreams "Mad Behind the Set Kale Sound"—Friday 5th—Una was/ Funk d'void—Techno meets funky jazzy house meets Glasgow Funk d'void/Grand Master Flash "immortalized by Blondie, feted by the hip-hop cognoscenti, Grand Master Flash turned the humble record deck into an instrument as potent as the piano or guitar"/Afrika Bambaata. B.Boy and Dance classics Saturday 29th (Mancccc Wabanakkk) . . .[88]

The energy of assembly in these notices exhibit a funk imaginary, a poetic expression which makes its world act with harmony. It is devoid of the language of advertisement but operates within its frame; the inventory resembles the surrealist technique of bricolage but grooves to the fantasies of Black music—which, to borrow language from Brand on jazz, is to say that the visual experience of the list "leaves [us] open, and up in the air and that this is the space that some of us need, an opening to another life tangled up in this one but opening."[89] The inventory ushers us (to return us to Benjamin's language for advertisement) into a dreamworld, but this one not of cuddly capitalism. Here "Grand Master Flash turned the humble record deck into an instrument as potent as the piano or guitar." In other words, this ethical and aesthetic commitment to innovation and reinvention, this opening to another life tangled up in the immediate confine, is the queer cuddle that funks the hold.

There is an enigma, a quandary of sorts in the inventory of these Black cultural forms, in how the names of albums and people and places are connected through juxtaposition, cutting across musical genres as well as racial, ethnic, and class lines. And yet, when read as an aural "map" to Black compositions,[90] the inventory strings hooks to another place in the Black Atlantic simply because of the intersubjective position (in the hold) of being and becoming in composition; choreographing this across artistic practices reroutes thinking into a funky practice. It allows us to see the kinds of being and becoming that might be possible in such political composition.

The play in these funky compositions makes me feel less jiggy with the who and where and what in Black compositions (some I knew, some I searched, some remain unknown). It makes me more excited to get down into the patterns in the loops of DJs, turntablists, trumpeters, blues guitarists, jazz vocalist, rappers, producers, and remix artists grooving in the compound of the page. There is rupture in this cuddle funk mixtape; it instantiates an Afro-modernity that is openly multidimensional and multilingual, and that celebrates the sounds of a global Black world. When the enslaved bump against each other, they ground faith in each other, and in the funk of each other. This devotion is not for a propositional end. It is a dream-prayer with ruptural energies. It creates and constitutes the gift that it proposes to give. *That*, too, is part of the relational capacities of funk.

The statue of Theodore "Teddy" Roosevelt, flanked by Black and Indigenous figures, by James Earle Fraser that was erected in front of New York City's Natural History Museum in 1939. Thanks to years of protest, it was removed in 2022 and its present fate is being debated. Photograph 2015 by Edward H. Blake via Flickr under Creative Commons (CC BY 2.0).

Bearing

*In which our author asks us to critically embrace the
teddy bear with its legacies of race and settler colonialism and asks us to consider how the cuddly and the cute
are by no means innocent social constructions.*

Why do I turn to the improvisatory laws of
funk that thanks to the DJs, spins us out of false
reassurances? How else to navigate the loaded
violence that lurks in the calculating hands of
capitalism and the states that hold us in the continuous present other than to experiment with the
gravity of what could be? Bearing that in mind,
and being free of the illusion that cuddling is only
innocent, we can continue our genealogy of the
racial embrace.

Many of us learn to cuddle not only from those
humans who raise us but also from a strange surrogate: an intimate toy, a soft simulacrum. The
most famous of these in the commodity age is the
teddy bear. It has a rather uncanny origin, involving a president's masculinity, a formerly enslaved
hunting guide, a near-dead animal, and a settler
colonial context. This story recalls how cuddling
can help us see how a white-supremacist world
choreographs Black people in scenes of subjection and atmospheres of death at the same time

as it crafts implicit and explicit narratives (some-times encoded in material culture, as you shall see here) that hide and or displace responsibility. As the story goes, in November 1902, only 14 months after he had taken the 26th presidential oath of office, Theodore "Teddy" Roosevelt travelled to Mississippi to participate in a recreational hunt for a black bear, an indigenous species that was quickly becoming endangered by human preda-tion and habitat destruction.[91] Desperate to find a specimen for the president to shoot, his hired hunting guide, a freed Black man and confed-erate veteran, Holt Collier, managed to capture an old, lame, undersized bear and bind it to a tree. But Roosevelt, who had campaigned on the strength of his public image as a rugged Ameri-can sportsman, was disgusted at the idea of killing the pathetic beast, and the bear was mercifully released back into the woods. In spite of his love of hunting—and killing—Theodore Roosevelt, we are led to believe, despised the slaughter of innocent animals.[92]

As this bear story became a myth, it portrayed a president gentler than the one-time arch-col-onist roughrider and veteran of the merciless Spanish-American War who was indelibly asso-ciated with hypermasculine white supremacist jingoism.[93] Clifford Berryman, a political cartoon-ist for the *Washington Evening Star*, cranked out a drawing depicting Roosevelt, the great hunter, standing front and center with a visibly grate-ful black bear in the background. Gradually the cartoonist reduced the bear to a cuddly cub tied up behind a campfire, with no sign of Collier. In turn, Morris Michtom, a Brooklyn candy-store owner, and his wife Rose, who specialized in making plush animals, started mass producing toy bears. With the president's permission, they named this commodity the "teddy's bear,"[94] a term that soon became synonymous with comfort, love, and childhood itself. The cuteness of the teddy bear lays bare how that which is dangerous is domesticated, obfuscating the compulsive political violence of making a being, this bear, vulnerable. The teddy bear becomes a surrogate for a human cuddler.

On the one hand, the surrogate force of the teddy bear's trademark power to lend comfort echoes the commercial arrangement of surrogacy, where a person lends their womb to assist in reproduction. This commercial arrangement is far from innocent of racial politics.[95] On the other, it anticipates the birth of the boutique "cuddling industry," in which entrepreneurs offer group workshops or one-on-one sessions for what is presented as an explicitly non-sexual experience of embodied intimacy.[96] It also indexes the rise of children's commercial culture and advertising: the teddy bear was one of the first "fads" or "must-have" toys. It was also one of the first to make extensive use of advertising, a graphic tradition that emerged, as we have seen, with images like that of *Brookes* and that, in the period of the teddy bear's origin, was built on racial imagery, notably the "cuddly" figure of Aunt Jemima.[97] Importantly, the teddy bear emerged at a moment when American views and anxieties about childhood were at a crossroads as public education and laws preventing certain forms of cruelty to certain children (and other forms of state cuddling) were being propounded around a highly racialized and gendered theory of innocence. Advertising and the growing market for mass-produced toys benefited from and participated in these anxieties.

President Roosevelt's teddy bear story requires my bringing into intimate dialogue the worldmaking horrors of settler colonialism and slavery, as opposed to subordinating one to the other.[98] Such a subordination tends to obscure "an illuminating blackness or redness," and tends to contribute to what Charles Mills sees as the "flourishing White ignorance."[99] To subordinate one to the other is a stance of nonrelationality, of not reading the work in Black and Indigenous studies, and, as a result, of not attending to the variegated historical events that inform their encounters with one another and with various European empires and empires of thought.

Returning to the famous cartoon, Roosevelt, the archetype of settler masculinity, refuses to succumb to barbarism and kill the decrepit creature, making him the "protector" not only of this indigenous animal but also of an American civilization, now framed through him as strong but fair, rugged but merciful. But behind the story is a formerly enslaved Black man who had been financially retained to find the master hunter something to kill. Thus, the settler colonial tale is also one of racial capitalism. What is being reiterated, symbolically and materially, when we, the descendants of these characters, cuddle the teddy bear, the descendant of that poor animal? What is being reproduced when we raise children, literally and metaphorically, to embrace it, physically and imaginatively, as a surrogate?

Scholars of imperialism have shown that at the heart of both game hunting and empire is a patriarchal claim to possess land and the lives upon it. In *Fencing the Forest: Conservation and Ecological Change in India's Central Provinces, 1860–1914*, Manesh Rangarajan argues that colonial officials largely equated "recalcitrant wild animals," such as bears and tigers, with rebels or "disobedient human beings," justifying their elimination whenever possible in the name of enlightened ecological stewardship.[100] In *Empire of Nature*, John MacKenzie argues that European recreational hunting in Africa and Asia marked colonial "dominance of the environment" while also constructing British imperial masculinity around a myth of self-sufficiency.[101]

What, then, are we to make here of Holt Collier, the silenced Black guide, employed to tap his intimate knowledge of the bear's ways to secure a sacrifice for Roosevelt's performance of masculinity? His mastery had to be erased to make way for the president's story. In contrast to Daniel Boone or Davy Crockett's legendary reputation as bear hunters and frontiersmen, few remember Collier's name. According to the Smithsonian, Collier was "credited with killing over 3,000 bears—more than the number taken by Daniel Boone and Davy Crocket put together."[102] This success invites us to engage with both the racial complicities constitutive of the processes of settler colonialism and the near-extinction of these bears thanks to hunting and habitat loss. To invoke Jodi Byrd, we should listen for the racial and colonial cacophonies that sound from Collier's biography.[103]

For example, James Matthews' 2017 documentary on Collier's life foregrounds traces of his transformation from an enslaved young boy into a runaway slave into an orderly at a hospital into a Confederate military marksman in the Civil War into a cowboy into an entrepreneur (providing/selling food to laborers at the Mississippi Delta levee camps and Mississippi Delta railroad camps during the nineteenth century) into a sought-after hunting guide.[104] On two different occasions, 1902 and 1907, he instructed the president on how to hunt for the increasingly elusive Black bears in the Mississippi Delta, the last area in the United States where the animals could be found in large numbers. Black life here wiggles under the weight of the forms of social vulnerability built by the racial and colonial settler state, and it lives through improvisation.

Commenting on Collier's economic life, Dr. Rolando Herts, director of Delta Center for Culture and Learning at Delta State University, identifies him as a wealthy man for this time. He was able to make $2,000–3,000 a year, during a hunting season, mostly through satisfying white clients' wish to embrace adventure. Hank Burdine, a historian interviewed in the documentary, points out that Collier identified himself as a veteran of the Confederate 9th Texas Cavalry until the day he died in 1936. Matthews' documentary goes on to identify Collier as the first sportsman of African descent to receive national fame. James Cummins, the executive director of Wildlife Mississippi and vice president of Boone and Crockett Club, identifies Collier as a progenitor of the principal of fair chase (a tenet trademarked by the Club, of which Teddy Roosevelt was the founder). The principle dictates that game animals be "wild" and free-ranging and sets out rules for their honorable slaughter. In the shadows of the fair chase principle lurks the history of American hunting and tracking which destroyed Indigenous people's food systems, the legacy of the slave patrols and anti-"Indian" gangs from which today's police forces were forged. The principle of fair chase, then, recalls fugitivity and its policing. In 2003, The Holt Collier National Wildlife Refuge became the only such site to be named in honor of an African American.

Collier's story illuminates the fractured continuities of slavery, conquest, and settler colonialism that are silent in the teddy bear's story. That is to say, this settler colonial object is stuffed with varied and various messy archives.

The settler masculinity of game-hunting bears traces to the masculinity of today's gay cultures, where the animal kingdom has become a filtering device on platforms like Grindr, gay Tinder and other dating and hook up apps. We can observe this gay worldmaking in, for example, the "tribes" feature of one's Grindr profile, which enables one to identify what kind of man one is or that one wishes to pursue, bears and otters, foxes and wolves. The zoological features of the totemic animal is used to mark the physical features of a man's body: its size, hairiness, and fitness.[105]

Interestingly, rugged is its own tribe, not a quality mapped onto the bear.

That carnal desire is managed through zoological rhetoric points to the microphysics of queer relations, and to how queer desires tend to play outside of regulated lines. For example, part of what makes the "cuddly" aspect of gay bears stand out is its juxtaposition with "rugged," which is coded as aggressive and hypermasculine. Though there are those who identify or are identified as hybrid "rugged bears," the tribes are distinct. Bear culture organizes masculinity around pride in rejecting the conventional associations of desirability with slimness and fitness and, more generally, refusing to homogenizing standards of physical masculine beauty. It celebrates somatic diversity centered on bulky men with huggable mass that Rebecca Popenoe, mobilizing her ethnographic experience among the Mauritanian Moors to write on fat-as-beauty, argues offers lovers "something to hold on to."[106] This *something*, for me, is more than the folds of skin; it represents a refusal to disavow the old, lame, undersized bear, to embrace animality by re-inscribing unconditional desirability into a figure of conditional desirability. By avowing human animality, it invites an ecological meditation on the theaters of settler masculine performance and it politicizes the intimacy between queerness and ecology.

Roosevelt's legacy of masculine persona, as a big game hunter, is linked to the huggable toy that we snuggle. We have the state-father producing a surrogate for us to bond with. We see ways that hunting, an activity laced with desires for possession, is a structured seduction that links race, sensuality, sexuality, and animality together. And we also see the entanglement between the violence and intimacy that the aggressive, insecure masculinity of bourgeois Americans made possible in the imperial age of world wars. That bears "stay" rugged even while cuddling unsettles cuddling as a tender-full act free from ruggedness, thus calling on us to attend to the rough, careworn topographies of the practices of cuddling, inviting meditations on who gets to cuddle and (still) be rugged. This should amplify what critics of masculinity have known for a long time: hegemonic and subordinate masculinities are not polar opposites.[107]

Returning to the tale of the teddy bear, I recall anthropologist Claude Levi-Strauss's assertion that "animals are good to think with,"[108] a claim which acknowledges the ability of human to metaphorically or anthropomorphically project human ideas and feelings onto animals, in particular ideas and feelings that cannot otherwise be directly acknowledged or contended with directly. So too for empires. The tropical "fieldwork" of the Smithsonian-Roosevelt African Expedition of 1909 led to the establishment of the National Museum of Natural History in New York.[109] It was initially proposed by Roosevelt, who had just finished his second term as president, and was staffed by naturalists selected by the Smithsonian, which also raised the funds for the project. In his book *African Game Trails,* Roosevelt remarks that "few laymen have any idea of the expense and pains which must be undergone in order to provide groups of mounted [e.g. taxidermied] big animals from far-off lands, such as we see in museums."[110] These stuffed, once-living animals, who now inhabit the silenced halls of the museum on stolen Lenape land, are part of the childhood memories of many of the luminary New Yorkers who would become foundational to twentieth-century culture, science, and capitalism, brought there by parents and teachers to learn about the world in the embrace of the institution. They would have walked past the bronze statue of Roosevelt on horseback at the entrance, flanked by a Native American and an African figure; in 2020, the 80-year-old statue, originally composed to mark the subjugation of these two figures, was removed in response to vigorous protests.[111]

The contemporary news about Roosevelt's "scientific" expedition, as well as subsequent exhibitions of its prizes, contributed to, as Elizabeth Hanson argues, "Americans considering Africa as the 'world's zoo.'"[112] Having been excluded from the scramble for African territory that culminated in the 1884–5 Berlin Conference, the American settler colony, built with enslaved African labor, had to make do with its commercial empire and its menagerie of stuffed animals. These helped to cement in the imagination the association of Africa and Africans with a spectrum of animality, ranging from the cute to the laughable, the curious to the lethal. In the white imagination, Africa and Africans embraced and were embraced by all these animal qualities at once.

Roosevelt returned from his 1902 bear hunting expedition with Collier determined to place America's "natural treasures in a protective embrace." His efforts led to the development of the United States' National Park system, a process that included the forcible embrace of many Indigenous territories, foreclosing and rescripting the intimacies of the human and non-human that had been practiced there for millennia. Whether read as the laboratory for the nation or the nation's repository of historical memory, the park system and the museum highlight the intimate syncopation between ecology and empire. And, interestingly, it is from the figure of Teddy Roosevelt, the generous reformer, the sophisticated diplomat, the cultured man of letters, the rough Darwinist, the harsh eugenicist, the ruthless imperialist, that we get the figure of the teddy bear, the love object of children and adults alike.

How do we bear this story in the way we embrace and are embraced? How does this history bear down on us with a weight that comforts some and crushes others? How does this archive express itself in our bearing, in the comportment of bodies that are read as responsible or threatening, entertaining or unbearable, full of life or marked for death? It is into the thick of these questions we turn.

Panda Ross performs Sam Cooke's "Bring it on home to me" on *X-Factor*, Season 2 in 2012.

Attraction and Abjection

*In which our author, taking up a performance on the hit
TV talent show X-Factor, advises the reader of the ways
in which Black women's queer, cuddly corporeal surplus
is the subject of both desire and derision, celebration and
incarceration.*

In a memorable 2012 scene that won her many
fans, Panda Ross, a 42-year old Black woman from
Dallas, Texas, auditioned for *The X-Factor USA* with
a stirring performance of Sam Cooke's "Bring It
On Home To Me." Panda walks on stage, a bejew-
eled necklace reading "single" hanging above the
standard-issue six-digit contestant number fixed
to her wide chest, surely reminding many viewers
of a prison identification tag. She responds to the
"hello" of celebrated acerbic reality-TV anti-hero
and *X-Factor* judge Simon Cowell with an infec-
tious smile, fangirling, with a "Hi Simon." She
irreverently informs him "I'm your baby mama,
you're my boo . . . I wore this necklace which says
single just for you." She explains: "I fought my way
to get here. I've been sick with . . . pneumonia; I
just got out of the hospital yesterday after seven
days; but I wasn't going to let nothing hold me
back from seeing you." She invites the audience
to take pleasure in the excess flirtatiousness, refus-

ing the comfortable image of the sexless Big Black Woman. Her playfully performed hyper-visible Black female sexual eroticism received collective laughter. "Well, I admire that," Simon says in response to her and proceeds to ask the customary first question, "So, what's your name?" "Panda," she responds. "What?" Simon asks. Emphatically, she states. "Panda. Like the bear." As the camera ping-pongs between them, you hear a titillated audience hollering with laughter. "That's your name?" Simon asks. "That's my real name," she responds. "Why were you called Panda?" Simon inquires further. "My mom, well she was kinda, you know, in jail when she had me, and her cell-mate was a white lady, she was Black. And so they just kinda came up with the name . . ." Two of the other panel judges (Demi Lovato and L.A. Reid) cover their faces and move uncomfortably in their chairs, displaying shock and surprise. The image cuts to Panda's young daughter and son, backstage, smiling/smirking at the erotic spectatorship of the audience and judges. Simon flirts with Panda: "Well, you never know, I love Pandas, so who knows." Panda doesn't miss a beat: "and I'm cuddly and everything, you know."

Deploying the aesthetic form of reality TV series' participatory grammar of flirtation, Simon and Panda game the wandering grammar of flirtation. Through this mode of engagement, some viewers might see the economy in their flirtation as "almost-nothing" while others, like me, might read "almost-everything" into it.[113] The choreography in their flirtation, the back and forth transgressions, tilts me into Hortense Spillers argument that the standard grammatical distinctions, as well as standard psychoanalytic stories about the psychic investment in grammars of kinship, desire, and gender identity, are rendered incoherent by the practice and the aftermaths of antebellum slavery. Bear with my leap. When Panda enters, as she does, and the judges and audience evaluate her performance, as they do, the staging of the show puts the judges in a role akin to an appraising buyer at the slave auction. Here's a woman entertaining with her voice (which requires the use of her lungs) while recovering from a respiratory illness, one that disproportionately kills Black Americans. What is it that we learn from Salman Rushdie's "At the Auction of the Ruby Slippers," a short story in which all sorts of people turn out to watch the bidding on Judy Garland's famous footwear from the 1939 film, *The Wizard of Oz*: "It is to the Auctioneers we go to establish the value of our pasts, of our futures, of our lives."[114] [What is it that Dorothy says? "There's no place like home"]. What is the grammatical, social, and psychic framework that will make sense of Panda's performance as a recreation of the auction block, and in relation to which Panda may make sense of herself?

As Panda prepares to sing, L.A. Reid confides to his fellow judges, and of course to the participating audience, that he "can't get past the name." But fellow judge Britney Spears does not join in the joke and stares (in a way some might describe as visibly uncomfortable) at the aspiring star, perhaps considering Panda's virtuosic labor in fulfilling the fantasy of *The X-Factor USA* audience, or perhaps recognizing the knowledge-vulnerability in what she has shared.

And with that, Panda soulfully sings the first three verses of Cooke's "Bring It On Home To Me." *I know I laughed when you left, But now I know I only hurt myself.* She earns the applause of the audience and a prized *yes* vote from all four judges. *You know I'll always be your slave, 'Til I'm buried, buried in my grave.* Not only was she approved to participate in the next round of the competition, her audition was also televised, winning her many fans that would see her returned to the show in a later season, even though she would not ultimately win that year's competition.

Panda's embodiment of Black women's erotic/ sensual joy is, in the popular white-supremacist imagination, the flip side of Black women's public grief that has come to mark them, in mourning, as strong and resilient. I have in mind Eric Garner's daughter, or Trayvon Martin's mother, or Mike Brown's or George Floyd's female kin and the way their grief was politicized. Or we might also point to the front-page images of Black women's grief, notably Etta James, at the 1964 funeral of Sam Cooke who, at 33, was killed by a motel manager in what many at the time believed to be a conspiracy against the celebrity advocate for civil rights.[115]

Panda's nuanced performance of fat Black female erotic agency allows us to meditate on the methods of critique that cuddling also requires of us. The regimes of heteropatriarchy, misogynoir, anti-fatness, capitalism, and settler colonialism might each offer analytics through which to read the dramas that shape this performance. For us not to read them along and against the grain of each hermeneutic is to adapt to the silences around Black women's erotic subjectivity and sexualities. Such an attitude would have intense consequences for Black women because of the relationship of their sexuality to colonial power. This kind of reading moves us away from what Jennifer Nash characterizes as the "[B]lack women have it bad" discourse, and from legacies of racialized exploitation and sexual violence, which not only make a spectacle of suffering, they emerge out of and contribute to the presumption that Black women can, should or must suffer. Instead, Nash argues we ought to orient our readings to the "sexual and erotic pleasures in racialization, even when (and perhaps precisely because) racialization is painful."[116]

On the grounds of Black cultural production and queer optics, rumors of queerness and same-sex erotics have circulated around big-figured Black rappers, including Lizzo, Missy Elliot, and Queen Latifah. As such, I want to undertake a queer reading of Panda's performance, attending to its range of desires. Let us be mindful of John Nguyet Erni's advice when he writes "the queer body is an adventure in surplus representations":[117] it refuses containment. All the residual effects that lie outside of assumed intentions and "official" meanings proscribed to the music, to her Blackness, to her femininity, to her body size, to her sensuality, the surplus in Panda's performance: this is what positions this performance as a queer act. More than that, the experience of being Black, particularly of being a Black woman, negotiating the (lethal, joyful, ambivalent) inheritances of modernity, is itself an adventure in surplus, in excess representation. Panda's cuddliness is brash, ecstatic, and interlinks Black erotics and humor. In this subversive dependence on humor, we see what Nash means when she argues that "race is an erotic project."[118]

The performance Panda delivers embodies a crisis in the representational contours of the big Black female entertainer that is, having been instilled by popular culture, often ubiquitous in our social imaginaries. In *Fearing the Black Body: The Racial Origins of Fat Phobia*, Sabrina Strings connects anti-fatness and anti-Blackness by linking "a fetish for svelteness and a phobia about fatness" to "the spread of Protestantism" that preached austerity and to the "rise of the transatlantic slave trade," when "[r]acial scientific rhetoric about slavery linked fatness to 'greedy' Africans."[119] Attending to the misogynoir of anti-fat discourses, Strings situates "the rise of the big [B]lack woman" in the long eighteenth century, when the mythical idleness of Africans was reinforced by depictions of African women. This notably included the 1810 public touring exhibition of Saartjie "Sara" Baartman, billed as the "Hottentot Venus" whose audiences were titillated by the disclosure that she possessed the "kind of shape which is most admired among her countrymen."[120]

I admire Panda's ingenuity in positioning herself as an economic actor within the neoliberal capitalist economic structures of the X-Factor competition. In her hustle to seek fortune and fame, she deals the hand she was played. Panda's biographical narrative concerning the genesis of her name, and her assertion that she wasn't "going to let nothing hold [her] back, from seeing [Simon]" challenges the ideological norms of the show. There is a queer pleasure in watching and listening to Panda flirt with Simon, whose celebrity stems from his caustic and austere untouchability and unfiltered judgments. Her assertive cuddliness envelopes him. I am also drawn to the fields of play that her performance "produces." Julia Himberg and Lynne Joyrich argue that the queer televisual spectacle "produces a tension between the articulation of the mainstream and, at the same time, the unsettling of the mainstream, both framing and displacing a televisual logic as it attempts to take queer viewers and issues into account, even as it aims to undermine TV's usual accounting."[121] I would add: racialized queer readership/viewership mandates a reevaluation of how audiences read cultural texts.

Taken as a complete performance, Panda prefaces Sam Cooke's song about home, betrayal, and heartbreak with a narrative about incarceration and the queer potential of the Black mother, thus foregrounding ways Black bodies have always existed in tension with normative gender.

In this sense, Panda Ross's performance interrupts the regularly scheduled program of *The X-Factor USA*. The story Panda tells about her name invites us to grapple with the fact that (1) her imprisoned pregnant mother gave birth to her in jail; (2) the biography of her name foregrounds a history of mass state incarceration and the role the state plays in producing conditions in which adults and children experience parental incarceration; (3) confining a pregnant Black woman in a jail cell sediments the cuddlespace of the hold in the continuous present. These facts prompt us to question how the increasing incarceration of Black women demands that we attend to the heteronormative imperatives of the incarceration system within which Panda was born and where she was first cuddled by the hold of the state. In using the history of her name to make Black maternal incarceration visible, Panda reveals the work of the cuddle undercommons. She also does this through the presence of her children by her side at the audition, challenging the popular narrative that children of incarcerated parents will also become incarcerated.

We should contend with the queer and social reproductive work that mates inside the walls of cell blocks do. Panda's mom's and her white cellmate "lady" ceremoniously invent her name, demonstrating the ways spaces of legal confinement are key state institutions of social and racial intimacies. While the narrative of Panda's name induces laughter, the scandal in the laughter has more to do with the unease at the intimacy between these women and the ease with which Panda narrates it: Here, the lawbreakers held in custody, who are queered, are loved rather than pathologized. Yet as we shall see in the next chapter, Panda's virtuosity takes place in a context where the punitive carceral mode of "state cuddling" that embraced her mother and delivered her to this world has in many ways been replaced by a neoliberal mode, where spectacular competitions like *X-Factor* offer the promise of care based on individual ambition and entrepreneurialism, where cuddliness can be rendered an asset. Yes, the big Black woman is cuddly, as Panda confirms. But this cuddly body is not a docile body open to subjection by colonial, imperial, and even microbial powers; rather, she asserts the lifeforce of erotics—Panda's desires, unholdable.

When she asserts her desire and says to Simon, "I'm cuddly and everything," Demi Levato, one of the female judges, responds with "Awwww," a response often reserved for children or animals, evoked by harmless cuteness. Yet when Panda reveals the jail as the source of her birth and name, Levato is shocked, bringing her palms first over her mouth, then to her cheeks. I take this "I can't believe the horror of this narration" gesture as signaling the "talent" show's capitalization of personal tragedy. If we can do away with the idea that the celebrity judges are moved purely by human sympathy, at least part of the horror is the intrusion of the incarcerated Black prisoner (or her child) into a space where it ought not appear. If, etymologically, interest means "to be in-between," then the judges' interest in Panda, this cuddly Black woman, lies somewhere in between abjection and affection. Or, putting the emphasis a little differently, what lies between Panda and the judges (and the audience?), linking them in unstable ways, is an emotional terrain in which affection and abjection are always shifting and swirling into and out of each other in the racial embrace.

Continuous Present

his driver's license	your gun
his toy gun	your gun
his BB-gun	your gun
his toy gun	your gun
his toy gun	your gun
his toy gun	your gun
his cellphone	your gun
his cigarettes	your gun
his BB-gun	your gun
his bottle of Buttons	your gun
his underwear	your gun
his car keys	your gun
his Bible	your gun
his Skittles	your gun
his cellphone	your gun
his screwdriver	your gun
his wallet	your gun

his driver's license

　　　your gun

　　　　　my boarding pass

07 26 16

his toy gun

　　　your gun

　　　　　my umbrella

01 06 15

his BB-gun

　　　your gun

　　　　　my scandal bag

03 29 15

his toy gun

　　　your gun

　　　　　my remote control

07 25 15

his toy gun

　　　your gun

　　　　　my Zipsor

10 20 15

his toy gun

　　　your gun

　　　　　my flashlight

11 15 15

his cellphone

　　　your gun

　　　　　my gum

12 31 15

his cigarettes

　　　your gun

　　　　　my glove

07 17 15

his BB-gun

　　　your gun

      my iPod

                    11 22 14

his Oxycodone

    your gun

        my hood

                    12 02 14

his underwear

    your gun

        my razor

                    04 08 13

his car keys

    your gun

        my breath mint

                    07 28 13

his Bible

    your gun

        my Quran

                    02 07 12

his Skittles

    your gun

        my pen

                    02 22 12

his cellphone

    your gun

        my slice of pizza

                    03 24 12

his screwdriver

    your gun

        my toothbrush

                    01 22 11

his wallet

    your gun

        my pick

                    02 04 99

4 bullets	your gun
7 bullets	your gun
I bullet	your gun
20 bullets	your gun
12 bullets	your gun
15 bullets	your gun
5 bullets	your gun
1 bullet	your gun
1 bullet	your gun
2 bullets	your gun
1 bullet	your gun
5 bullets	your gun
3 bullets	your gun
1 bullet	your gun
1 bullet	your gun
2 bullets	your gun
19 bullets	your gun

On Cuddling

Phanuel Antwi

nutritionist and   your gun
truck driver and   your gun
security guard and   your gun
mechanic and   your gun
armed robber and   your gun
handy man and   your gun
father and   your gun
gardener and   your gun
sketch artist and   your gun
operator and   your gun
street peddler and   your gun
hacker and   your gun
soldier and   your gun
footballer and   your gun
entrepreneur and   your gun
mechanic and   your gun
his wallet   your gun

my driver's license	your gun
my toy gun	your gun
my BB-gun	your gun
my toy gun	your gun
my toy gun	your gun
my toy gun	your gun
my cellphone	your gun
my cigarettes	your gun
my BB-gun	your gun
my bottle of pills	your gun
my underwear	your gun
my car keys	your gun
my Bible	your gun
my Skittles	your gun
my cellphone	your gun
my screwdriver	your gun
my wallet	your gun

On Cuddling

Phanuel Antwi

VAG
ABO
NDS

State Cuddling

In which our author proposes to reframe the continuous present of structural and systemic anti-Black violence, as mediated by government and its institutions, as state cuddling, with special attention to the situation of Black women.

It is not uncommon to be loved to death. Men who murder intimate partners and their children are often heard to say that they "loved them too much" (to allow a divorce, to allow a daughter to date "one of them," to allow a son to be gay, or a daughter to become a son). Since the beginning of the global racial project, even prior to the invasion of the Americas in 1492, European elites have entitled themselves as father figures to many others and entitled themselves to an often-lethal form of care. From the Pope's fatherly "protection" of Indigenous Americans to slaveholders' claims (still echoed today) that the people they held in bondage were "like family," the history of racial capitalism contains many crushing embraces.

In this chapter, I turn to what I am calling state cuddling to describe how this phenomenon plays out through police and policy. When sharpened to a point, state cuddling helps us name what inspires and enables agents of the state—from police officers to those who deputize themselves to do the work of the police—to crush life from Black men in chokeholds. But in a more ambient sense, state cuddling is everywhere and nowhere at once, a force of coercive care that suffocates Black life. In this chapter, I am drawn to a particular transition in state cuddling that spans the post-Civil Rights era and the neoliberal era, a period of deindustrialization and the hyperpolicing of Black people in the United States and elsewhere.

How to account for this, or render an account of it? Is there a cuddling social scientist among us? Or, are we all literary and cultural studies cuddlists? I ask these questions because I find myself wanting to handle data, to be handled by numbers, while, at the same time, asking: when has an empirical description or enumeration of Black suffering ever done anything for Black people, other than code, classify, and discipline Black life?

Social scientists are good at teaching us ways that practices and ideas change over linear time. They can help us track trends on graphs or periodize power; however, one thing that Black life knows, intimately, is the *continuous present* of living and dying. Moments nest and spoon into other moments in ways that defy comforting categories and seductive schema. Methodologically, this chapter departs from *cultural* objects to cuddle data, numbers, and dates. I begin by reflecting on Hortense Spillers' 1987 response to the 1965 US federal report on "The Negro Family: The Case for National Action," more commonly known as the *Moynihan Report*. In revisiting this infamous text in my own moment of the racial embrace, I want to draw attention to the spoonings of the continuous present: 2023, 1987, 1965 . . . this chapter asks what forms of care and coercion, of debt and discipline brood in these and other nesting dates. Yes, of course: between these dates we can observe a movement from liberal promises of state welfare to the neoliberal deputization of corporations as surrogate caretakers or caregivers. But even as we, along with Jackie Wang, attend to that transition toward "carceral capitalism," we must also read in Spillers disclosures about an "American grammar," the persistent syntax that embraces gender, race, and capitalism in a set of "symbolic substitutions."[122]

In considering state cuddling, I have in mind Gargi Bhattacharyya's discussion of "cuddly capitalism" in *Rethinking Racial Capitalism*, where she meditates on the promise that, for some, capitalism can appear to be a caring system, thanks in part to the tempering influence of the state. Yet as her analysis shows, there is something in what I am calling state cuddling that troubles the distinction between biopolitics and necropolitics, nesting one into the other so that the state can conceal its desires for unmediated force against populations it, itself, makes vulnerable and therefore racialized. As such, I am suggesting that what results as a marker of biopolitical practices in state cuddling is a matter of necropolitics at the same time that necropolitical practices openly embrace biopolitics. Some of those whom the state cuddles tenderly imagine that the welfare state is the vehicle for biopolitics and the "care" of the population. Some offer up tempting, comforting arguments that necropolitics are incidental, contingent and, at worst, temporary. I want to foreground ways that state cuddling also reveals how biopolitics and necropolitics lie side by side, at times cuddling one another: sometimes care is calculated to kill. Sometimes, hidden by the charisma of the state, there is a killability within biopolitics. In this way, state cuddling names a vestibular space, a threshold between biopolitics and necropolitics, where the state folds the past and future into the present in order to, on the one hand, enfold "exalted" racial subjects in the warmth of a mythical "then" while targeting the living lives of Black people in the "now."[123]

If we follow Spillers, we learn to apply gender as a lens to understand the paternalism of the racial state. So how then do we relate the state as parent to the American grammar book that "mark[s Black] wom[e]n" with names such as "'Peaches' and 'Brown Sugar,' 'Sapphire' and 'Earth Mother,' 'Aunty,' 'Granny,' 'God's 'Holy Fool,' a 'Miss Ebony First,' or 'Black Woman at the Podium'"[124] (or Panda on Stage)? How does the representation of Black women's parenthood become a state sanctioned role that Black women are rewarded to play for the benefit of the state, much like how children play house to feel in control? What is the relationship between the parenthood of Black women and that of the state?

For example, the investments we see in Daniel Patrick Moynihan's 1965 government Report "inscribes" Blackness, according to Spillers, "as a scene of negation."[125] Here is a (white) man who served as the Assistant Secretary of Labor for Policy Planning and Research for both President John F. Kennedy and Lyndon B. Johnson. Not only did his report propagate misogynoir, mobilizing postwar liberalism with its investments in mythologies of nation, of boot-strap economic mobility and individual moral superiority. Moynihan's report also used Black matriarchy as an argument against Black women. Here we see the differentiated ways patriarchy cuddles gender. The Report attributed the breakdown of Black family to the disempowerment of Black American men, who the report saw as not being able to support a typical patriarchal family. According to Moynihan:

> At the heart of the deterioration of the fabric of Negro society is the deterioration of the Negro family . . . In essence, the Negro community has been forced into a matriarchal structure which, because it is so out of line with the rest of American society, seriously retards the progress of the group as a whole, and imposes a crushing burden on the Negro male, in consequence, on a great many Negro women as well.[126]

Reading this Report, Spillers underscores what he missed when she suggests that "this stunning reversal of the castration thematic, displacing the Name and the Law of the Father to the territory of the Mother and Daughter, becomes an aspect of the African American female's misnaming."[127] In effect, Spillers argues that the Black woman has become nothing less than the "misnamed" agent of social pathology, castration, and human unbecoming in the troubled history of American democracy:

> We perceive that the dominant culture, in a fatal mis-understanding, assigns a matriarchist value where it does not belong; actually misnames the power of the female regarding the enslaved community. Such naming is false because the female could not, in fact, claim her child, and false, once again, because "motherhood" is not perceived in the prevailing social climate as a legitimate procedure of cultural inheritance.[128]

Against the premature closure that these responses provide to the historical "riddle" posed by Black womanhood, we can see ways that a figure like Panda is assigned a false script that she is con-scripted to perform. More than this, the report documented welfare dependency rates as well as high fertility rates as a sign of Black families' instability and insatiability. For Moynihan, Black Americans were trapped in a "tangle of pathol-ogy" on the ground, amd Moynihan's public policy believed military service would bolster African-American masculinity. Even though the rise of the Vietnam War after 1965 changed the context of the report, Moynihan believed soldier-ing paved a path for Black success as it had for himself and other white men who served during World War II.

This tangle that Moynahan called pathology has another face. It is the kind of mutual aid that anthropologist Carol B. Stacks calls "cooperative kin," based on her intimate study of two Black families (the Jacksons from Arkansas and the Waters from Mississippi) living in the poorest section of midwestern communities during the same time as the Report's emergence.[129] In *All Our Kin*, Stacks challenges Moynihan's controlling image of Black families as "deviant, matriarchal, and broken" by highlighting "the adaptive strategies, resourcefulness, and resilience of Black urban families under conditions of perpetual poverty" and "the stability of their kin networks."[130] This extensive collaboration in kin network is not dysfunctional. It is, as Stacks shows, the making of functional systems that supported Black people who are poor. The honest beauty in on-the-ground expressions of kinship not only improves the grooves of one's day-to-day existence but also rehearses the funky virtuosity of the hold.

How does the white, patriarchal state make a home of itself? In part through the identification and abjection of the Black maternal. What kind of home? Earlier, I underscored how, for many of us, home as cuddlespace can be or become a place of violation. Home is not always a garden to tend too tenderly. Sure, there are homes where you don't need to be clean to be welcomed. There are also homes where you learn to starve and thirst. There are homes that endeavor to take the architecture out of your spirit and leave a keen long ache to wage war on you. There are homes riddled with holes. Sometimes, the home you have left cannot shelter you from the storm of life that hurricanes in you. You come to accept there are warlords in every home, promising security. Some warm life when there is no moon. Others include

the presidents, the policymakers, the anchors that
weigh down life. They all make everyone's home.

Let us travel across the border to the Nova Scotia
Home for Colored Children ("The Home"). Why
make such a migration, in a book so far satisfied to
explore examples from the United States? Perhaps
because, from the vantage of the US, and among
its liberals and conservatives alike, Canada is presented as either heroically or despicably cuddly:
an allegedly functional welfare state, supposedly
unhaunted by a history of slavery and anti-Blackness. Yet it is precisely here that we can more
clearly observe the violence that looms over Black
hopes for state welfare, to be at home in the state.
I am pointing to the erasures necessary to hold
Canada up as exemplary of a welfare state that
"works." The space that these erasures leave open
are turned into cuddlespaces for the state to choke
lives it makes vulnerable.

The Home, located on a government-pur-
chased 85-hectare farm on Old Preston Road, 57
kilometers away from Canada's east coast government, military, and economic capital, Halifax,
opened in 1921 as a private child-caring institution for Black children whose needs were not
being met in a racialized society. The Home essen-
tially filled a gap in the provincial childcare system
as children of African descent were not welcome
in white institutions. While so often presented as
needy interlopers or the indebted refugees of the
Underground Railroad, Black people have been
an important part of Nova Scotia and broader
Canadian history since their earliest origins as
colonial settler states. And yet anti-Black violence

in these territories has always spooned with systematic neglect. As one former ward of "The Home" pointed out, the facility was "important because the Black kids, colored kids, as we said back then, weren't allowed in any other orphanages, and so they built their own." But over the years, the Home fell into disrepair and former residents suffered systemic and institutional racism, neglect, and abuse at the hands of staff. Government aid, necessary for any care facility that cannot rely on wealthy donors, was conspicuously scarce and government oversight was almost completely absent. Children were abused physically, mentally, emotionally, and sexually. The orphanage closed in the 1980s when stories from former residents began to emerge, shedding some light on the racism and racial segregation that existed at the time, prompting lawsuits, a settlement, and apologies. In 2014, then Nova Scotia Premier Stephen McNeil apologized on behalf of the government for the systemic racism that forced Black youth to be segregated to the former orphanage. This function of neoliberal apologies, of States owning up to the past (historical debt), ends up commercializing the apology for credit, and, given this tendency, must be tied to neoliberal economic reform. Much of what I narrate about this home parallels quite exactly the kinds of neglect and abuse reported in the Indian Residential School system. This approach to "schooling" and providing a "home" constituted a genocidal embrace for unwanted populations—a deliberate attempt to end the futures of Black and Indigenous children.

It is tempting to place the Moynihan Report or "The Home" in a history of the Welfare State that, however misguided, has been replaced by something worse: a neoliberal corporate state that has abandoned even the pretense of care and, instead, holds Black life in a tangle of forms of extraction and punishment, emblematized in Panda's own story, filled with scenes of incarceration and staged competition. And yet the continuous present of the racial embrace troubles such neat narratives. The Moynihan Report was already a response to the conditions of ghettoization, precariousness, and state abandonment that enfolded Black life in America well before it was systematized by the Chicago School in what would come to be known as neoliberalism in the 1970s and 80s. And yet that transition relied on ideological tropes cast in the "American grammar" I am associating with state cuddling, notably the figures of the "welfare queen" and the "nanny state."

The violence of history that makes me position state cuddling as the violence of state paternalism rubs against the work of policy researchers Julian Le Grand and Bill New, who account for both the successes and failures of government paternalism.[131] Their social scientific approach mobilizes the discourse of the nanny state as one pole of a debate between, on the one hand, conservatives who loath state assistance and intervention and, on the other, liberals, who see a place for it. The term first appeared in the British press in 1965, a few months after the publication of the Moynihan Report, and, thanks to arch-neoliberal politician Margaret Thatcher, became a catch-all phrase to deride the wasteful, meddlesome, and dangerous overreach of a government that takes too far its responsibility to care for the population.[132] And yet, I am interested in the racial register of the nanny, in ways that the material labor and resources of the nanny (including cuddling) condition the possibility for the state's very liberty. How does the nanny state require the care labor of Black women and other racialized women? The history of the Black nanny is different in the UK, where the term "nanny state" originated, than the story familiar in the US, with its iconography of Aunt Jemima. And yet the Jamaican nanny was a well-known and much debated figure in the England of the 1960s,[133] when the term was first coined. Around her revolved concerns about the nation-state's racial, gendered, and economic future.[134] In what they present as a reasoned analysis of the proper role of the welfare state, La Grand and New argue that, while the derisive accusations of state coddling are largely ideological, there is a role for state paternalism, and that welfare state entitlements and regulations must be measured against the use of more punitive prohibitions and other obstructions to individual liberty, which ought to be judged according to the *harm principle*, a concept imported from criminal law. The authors conclude that the state should be seen as a "helpful friend," not as a surrogate for individual decision-making. And yet whose friend is the state? To whom has the state been a friend? And what does such a language of friendship hide?

In contrast to La Grand and New's language of friendship, Lisa Lowe, in *The Intimacies of Four Continents*, scales intimacy by connecting the "archive of liberalism" (housed in the colonial state archives, from which intimacy has been traditionally separated) to the anticolonial intellectual traditions frequently considered alongside imperial ones. She does this to make legible the "modern fiction of progress and redemption" that the state tells itself.[135] The systemic and structural implication in Lowe's definition of "intimacy" is helpful here: at stake is "the affective medium for republican citizenship and the subject's felt sense of individual belonging in liberal society." For her the "fantasy, sentiment, and desire in literature and popular culture produce the contours of intimacy that mediate the individual's inhabiting of everyday life in social relations."[136] We see ways the soothing state wraps one arm around its citizens in a hugging embrace while the other hand chokes the life out of many of its subjects. Soothing is the reassertion of the state's presence in the lives of those vulnerable and dependent on its services.

In a neoliberal age of state cuddling, cuddling itself is drawn into the service of the state, which is now almost synonymous with the market. Corporate paternalism claims its inheritance. Since 2015, Cuddlist has provided an "international cuddling service with over 1,200 trained cuddliest practitioners who have completed over 15,000 sessions."[137] Cuddle Party Inc. is a "501(c)(3) nonprofit charitable organization" whose "mission and purpose is to promote and enable empowered consent, choice and nurturing touch . . . by training and certifying facilitators who produce Cuddle Parties and other related events."[138] Both emerge out of a new moment of "cuddly capitalism" that seeks to monetize and professionalize intimacies. While of course intimacy has always been part of the market, these initiatives resonate with or embody the logic of neoliberal self-investment. The language of the cuddle has also been important to new thinking within traditional corporations. Publisher Pan Macmillan proposes shifting the language of commerce from "marketing and publicity huddles," a phrase they use to communicate teamwork among different sectors of the company, to a "comms cuddle," a way for them to "suggest the idea of extending our arms around everything we do."[139]

It will come as little surprise that corporate cuddliness is also on the market for those forms of predatory financial extraction and debt-encumbrance that, as Denise Ferreira da Silva and Paula Chakravartty note, have come to define the economics of race in the neoliberal era and that led, so catastrophically, to the 2008 financial crisis.[140] The for-profit university system in the US is emblematic of this trend. Here, Black people and families are particularly targeted for predatory loans to empower them to "invest" in education toward degrees that rarely help materialize the jobs and security that such companies promise.[141] These predatory promises rehearse, in neoliberal form, the way that the state cuddling always already embraces Blackness in the continuous present.

For example, In a 2015 commercial featuring Black comedian and TV host Steve Harvey, we see him delivering a motivational speech to a room full of people, encouraging them to stop doing what they've been doing if they expect different results from their doings: "Make the decision to move your life forward, go to a place that can help you get it done, and go see what else life's got for you."[142] In a 2018 commencement address, Queen Latifah speaks to the graduates, predominantly Black, holding them up for their achievement and lauding the power of higher education for Black people.[143] The sponsor for these motivational speeches, featuring Black celebrities, was the US for-profit, accreditted degree-granting institution, Strayer University.

For-profit higher education comprises private institutions whose goals are to generate profit by offering post-high school credentials and degrees. This model of postsecondary education targets particular communities and industries, with the goal of *training* students for careers where there is demand. This is presented, in advertising and lobbying, as a personal student investment that can be recouped in the form of future wages. Institutions like Strayer have used such arguments not only to recruit student-customers but to secure access to US-government-backed student loans. Yet the reality is that the education these companies provide rarely leads to anything more than a life of debt, which actually increases the racial wealth gap.[144] For example, in Anna Louie Sussman's investigation on "The Effects of For-Profit Colleges on Student Outcomes and Debt," she found that most of these degrees "lower [the] likelihood of employment" and students "were less likely to be employed six years after graduation."[145]

Beyond such statistics, something more ideological is at work. We know from the liberation pedagogy of Paulo Freire that the "banking model" of education interpellates students into objects of knowledge,[146] and that this kind of banking pedagogy is a "bureaucratizing of the mind."[147] As Freire teaches us, banking education can "conceal certain facts which explain the way human beings exist in the world."[148] In banking on deregulation, one of the practices that the for-profit education institutions conceal is how they target jobless Black people to enroll, thereby sending Black folks into debt. In the training presentation for the now-shuttered for-profit Vatterrott College's recruiting officers, they identified the following as their preferred students: "Welfare Mom[s] with Kids," "Pregnant Ladies," "Recent Incarceration," and "Drug Rehabilitation."[149] In 2018, Vatterott was among the many for-profit universities that closed after it was discovered they had defrauded both students and the government.[150] Mike Brown, whose murder at the hands of Ferguson police in 2014 catalyzed the Movement for Black Lives, was scheduled to begin his education at Vatterott just two days later.[151] In the wake of that murder, it came to light that the municipality of Ferguson itself, like Vatterott, deployed a business model based on predatory fees and debts: its second largest source of revenue was fines levied by armed police, predominantly against its poor Black population.[152]

While the continuing insecurity of the economic crisis facing Black communities encourages
these targeted students to seek continuing education, Tiffany Dena Loftin, the National Director
for the NAACP Youth & College Division, informs
us that the cost of this education often means
many have to "mortgage their futures to pay for
college."[153] Loftin's use of the word mortgage
(in 2020) is haunted by the uneasy ghosts of the
subprime mortgage crisis of 2008, where many
Black people mortgaged their future. Here lies the
"racial/postcolonial, moral and economic refer-
ent, which," for Denise Ferreira da Silva and Paula
Chakravartty, "resolves past and present modali-
ties and moments of economic expropriation into
natural attributes of the 'other of Europe.'"[154]
That neither Chakravartty and Ferreira da Silva
or Loftin resolve the continuous presence of the
past and present and future invites us to link
the housing crisis to the student debt crisis, and
note how the continuous present of the financial
market not only hurts Black communities,[155] but
also we get to see ways that the continuous present
is an economic treadmill that mortgages the future
into the present.

The privatization of the educational market-
place finds echo in the operations of the criminal
justice system, where we also see the entanglement
of mass state incarceration and a privatized for-
profit industry. By now, many of us know that on
the other side of the for-profit education industry is the for-profit bail industry in the criminal
justice system. And, thanks to the work of thinkers such as Michelle Alexander's *The New Jim*

Crow and Alexes Harris' *A Pound of Flesh*, many of us also know that the fines and fees not only compound inequalities by turning poor people's assets into revenues for the state,[156] they are also among the ways that prisons generate profit.[157] Like Micoll Seigel, I am surprised to learn that "the bail bonds of people who go to prison are not cancelled."[158] Seigel's wonderful essay, "Hypothecation: debt bondage for the neoliberal age," scores the choreography between the state and the neoliberal market and helps me see the continuous entanglement of Black life in state and corporate apparatuses. That said, readers of Sadiya Hartman will recall that debt was a key means through which "the freed," following the Civil War and the sabotage of Black Reconstruction, were reinscribed into the hold of bondage, now in a financial and moral embrace.[159]

I return to the funk and soul in Panda's audition to suggest that franchises like *X-Factor* in some ways are deputized by the state to cuddle Blackness in coercive ways. In a neoliberal age of self-investment and competition, the show markets the possibility of self-marketing, making (predatory) promises not unlike those of for-profit colleges to reward hard work and discipline. In this case, the hard work is performing a hyperreal version of self on the televised social stage. I want to consider Panda's five-minute performance, particularly, her statement I wasn't "going to let nothing hold me back, from seeing [Simon]," as an assertion of her biopolitical right to exist by rising above her pneumonia. As such, I wish to read her performance as an articulation of a biography that productively challenges the (mis)conceptions of Black social and cultural life, particularly the iconographies of Black femininity from the grammar books that are suspended in the audience's psyche. The iconographies I have in mind are the untruthful "creation of four interrelated, socially constructed controlling images of Black womanhood" that Patricia Hill Collins identifies as "reflecting the dominant group's interest in maintaining Black women's subordination": the mammy, the matriarch, the welfare mother, and the Jezebel.[160] The long durée of these sociopathological names that are used to attack, abuse, and malign Black women work to "describe a locus of confounded identities, a meeting ground of investments and privations in the national treasury of rhetorical wealth."[161]

The particular type of Black femininity that Panda presents, which, in the popular imagination, gets her labelled as a sassy, unapologetic Black woman, is precisely the kind of femininity put on display to such catastrophic effect as the "welfare queen," a figure held up by right-wing politicians to justify the transformation of the overly cuddly welfare state into the punitive, carceral neoliberal entity we know today. Because the welfare queen was never a woman who was in the shadows, because she was someone proud of taking, Panda enters into a performance script already written. Her performance, on this reality show, is cloaked in a different order of reality performance designed by the state. Panda steps into a series of eras of the welfare queen as first proposed by the American national Hollywood father

Ronald Reagan and then carried out by another national Petro-liberator father, George Bush, and then revitalized by the cuddly national father, Bill Clinton, with his punitive welfare reforms. In some ways, this American grammar was normalized by a Black national father, Barack Obama, and, now, this Queen is dethroned by a new national father, Joe Biden, who, at one point, as senator under Clinton, helped coronate her through the welfare reform bill.

What Biden made official recently, in 2021, with the "American Rescue Plan," which includes what CNN journalist, John Blake, headlines as "Biden dethron[ing] the welfare queen,"[162] already happened years ago. It is within this narrative of rescuing, this fold of the American Dream, that the talent show as a genre emerges. When the parent abandons their responsibility for the child, displaces responsibility on to the child, and blames the child for its situation, it requires ingenuity on the child's part to survive; or, phrased differently, the condition of cruelty makes the child's ingenuity possible. Forms of cruelty take the shape of audition, competing, entertaining. The reward is the parent's attention and, if you're ultra-lucky, the parent's support. Franchises like *X-Factor*, which emerge along the lines of entrepreneurialism, take on the role of a neoliberal parent. It is no longer the government who takes care of the public. Individuals need to take care of themselves by developing their talents and putting themselves on the market; they need to embrace a sort of auto-entrepreneurialism. Such names do discursive damage to Black women, including

Panda, subordinating aesthetic joy and fugitivity to images of poverty and dependency. While tied to the modality of state cuddling embodied by police officers, what is different from the state cuddling in these repressive public polices is the state's deployment of controlling images and other discursive elements in public policy as expressions of government maternalism/paternalism. In other words, there lie social and ideological investments for the state behind the names used to describe Black women.

The above policies reveal what Melinda Cooper, in *Family Values: Between Neoliberalism and the New Social Conservatism*, theorizes: the political project of neoliberal thought is steeped in the idea of the "household" as its basic economic unit. We might add that this idea itself is steeped in the anti-Black weather of American racial capitalism. The state: a warlord who insists "my home is your home" and "your home is my home." The state claims the territory as its home and claims to protect the home. Operating on these scales, it is therefore not surprising that the state finds a way to cuddle us in its powerful embrace. We can recall Sweet Home, the iconic plantation of Toni Morrison's *Beloved*, first run by kindly whites who treat their slaves "like family," then by the sadistic schoolteacher. We can recognize the way the state sweetens itself, and on whose sugar. The dialectic of state regulation and intimate attachment (self-subjection to the neoliberal family) converges in state cuddling. While, in neoliberal times, this appears in the idiom of ruthless market competition (and its spectacular proxies like *X-Factor*), a longer view reveals that the racial capitalist state has never failed to crush Black life.[163]

With that in mind, we might now turn from state cuddling's slow strangulations to what the police and others euphemistically refer to as "sudden death," especially when it comes by their hands or the hands of those whom they deputize.

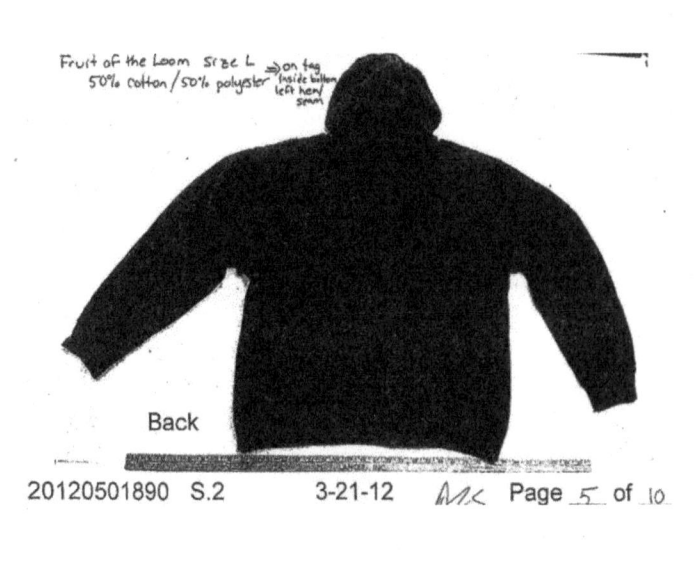

Fruit of the Loom Size L
50% cotton / 50% polyester → on tag inside bottom left hem/ seam

Back

20120501890   S.2   3-21-12   [initials]   Page 5 of 10

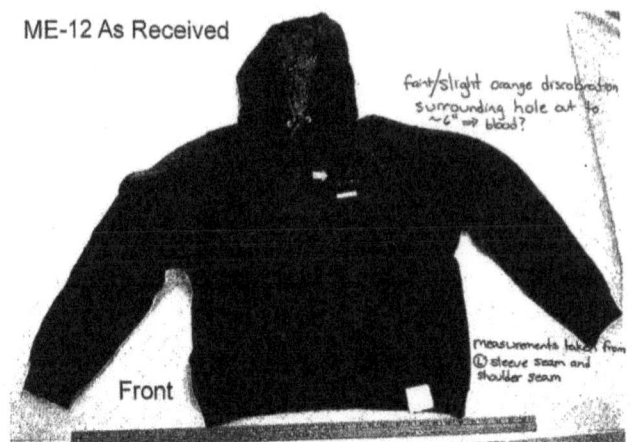

ME-12 As Received

faint/slight orange discoloration surrounding hole at ~6" ⇒ blood?

measurements taken from ℓ sleeve seam and shoulder seam

Front

Images of the hoodie Trayvon Martin was wearing when he was murdered, released by the Florida prosecutor's office in July of 2012.

VAG
ABO
NDS

Loved to Death

*In which our author, reflecting on children's toys and the
murder of children, notes that, as relates to Blackness, the
obverse side of cuteness is a license to cruelty.*

Sianne Ngai argues that there is "violence always
implicit in our relation to the cute."[164] There is
something in cuteness that simultaneously pro-
vokes both a disarming and doting affection, as
well as a desire to crush or throttle. Recognizing
this contradictory impulse allows me to under-
line how sometimes care can enable violence, or
how violence can stem from love, or how violence
can emerge from a genuine impulse to become
a savior. Captivity and comfort are often strange
bedfellows.

Trayvon Martin is being stalked, squiggly
grappled (embraced) and shot dead by George
Zimmerman, a townhouse neighborhood watch
coordinator in the Retreat at Twin Lakes, near
Orlando, Florida. In the aftermath, two images
circulated of 17-year-old Martin, whose crime
was to return from a local store with a packet of
Skittles in his clutching, while visiting his father's
fiancé in the gated community. In one, a smiling
Martin in a familiar red Hollister T-shirt grins at
the photographer. Incidentally, a shadowy figure

stands behind him, to his right, somehow amplifying his innocence. In the other, a pensive Trayvon, wearing a hoodie, stares downward into the lens of his phone; in the background institutional fluorescent lights are slightly distorted by the angle of the camera.

It may seem frivolous to attend to questions of fashion when addressing such events, but one simply needs to look at one of the first images that circulated after Trayvon's murder to understand how the public responded to the cuddly subject. To embrace this image of the all-American kid is, in many ways, to have Trayvon embrace us in return. Our mutual gaze offers a mutual embrace. The second image, of him in a hoodie, elicited a different response. While the hoodie led to his material demise, the jersey, emphasizing his Americanness, led to his symbolic cuddling. And yet, no clothing item feels more like it's cuddling you than the jersey hoodie.

There are many folds to the often-lethal cuddling of Blackness. So, before I continue unfolding the significance of the visual re-presentation of Trayvon Martin, let me pause on the cuteness of the self-contained enclave, the gated community, where he is being murdered, to meditate on another hold: the enveloping lens through which Black folks get captured in systems as a result of the logics of slavery and settler colonialism that architectures our everyday.

Of course, I have in mind the way that a long history of racism led to post-war "white flight" of the middle class to suburban gated communities, and also to the many ways Black people were excluded from buying into such fantasy zones, legally and culturally. One cannot avoid the way that American politicians throughout the late twentieth and still in the early twenty-first centuries, summon up the image of the Black "super predator" as the specter which threatens the sanctity of the gated enclave with theft, miscegenation, or declining property prices. Nor can one fail to link this to the long history of white vigilantism that, as Rinaldo Walcott shows, entitles itself to murder Black people to defend both the actuality and the principle of private property.[165]

But I am also after something else. Nestled in the ethos of the neighborhood watch is an idea that neighbors cuddle. I am not necessarily suggesting that neighbors physically hold each other. Rather, the neighborhood, in these communities, tends to organize itself around ideas of connections, given how houses are close, near, and next to each other; some houses, like the semi-detached townhouses at the Retreat of Twin Lakes, share walls, feeling their boundaries pressed up against others, folding an outside that operates within into deep relations. The spatial preposition of neighborly nearness, with riffed observations, extends the boundaries of a cuddle into the intimate realms of co-composition. Or, to think with Nahum Dimitri Chandler on the grammatical and syntactical force of prepositions, that neighbors cuddle is an "articulation of relations."[166] A fold, then, reveals more folds. In *The Fold: Leibniz and the Baroque*, Gilles Deleuze describes the "swarming" of folds.[167]

Folding takes on many meanings in the world of gambling, particularly in poker, where, through the course and rhythm of the game, a player displays character through the decision on whether they want to "hold'em" or "fold'em." Folding a hand of cards suggests withdrawal, but also taking a stance, one that is driven as much by rationality as it is by desires and emotions. The question of whether to fold or not to fold then requires discerning between knowing and doing.

Another fold. To be inside the fold of a flock not only means being birds of a feather but also sharing in the coordinated movements that form a murmuration, caught up in a feedback loop in the folds of a formation, a synchronized choreography. From the perspective of this group movement, Trayvon does not appear to the neighborhood watch to be wandering about as if separated from a flock of his neighbors (similar creatures) and seeking to return; instead, the eyes of the neighborhood watch are flocking around him and viewing him as prey to the flock or a predator.

What? Do we not "follow the fold up to the following fold"?[168]

The kinds of correspondence among neighbors I am calling cuddling, then, is not simply the choreographies that shape the architectural folds of a gated community. Nor am I simply bringing the architectural fold of the cuddle to bear on the architectural imaginary of the neighborhood watch; what I have in mind is the broad range of seams along the folds that offer places to gather. I am deconstructing architecture with Bernard Tschumi: "Buildings, in their simplest form, are made of vectors and envelopes."[169]

If we regard vectors and envelopes in terms of topography and inhabitation, the neighborhood watch operates as a seam that indexes and archives many gatherings. As a form of community care, neighbors keep watch over one another and participate in mutual aid, offering physical and social security in times of crisis. And yet, folded in this community service is a settler colonial form of care that manages space and race. The settler colonial surveillant grammar of the neighborhood watch is justifying surveillance, management, and dominance over this young Black boy. These grammars are reifying colonial mappings that associate Black masculinity, criminality, and unbelonging. They are figuring Trayvon Martin as a threat to neighbors and property. As Sara Ahmed writes in *Strange Encounters*, the threat "allows us to share a fantasy that, in the co-presence of strange and alien bodies, we will prevail."[170] This fantasy, perverse as it may be, secures the boundary-making of the neighborhood watch; it also reveals a set of vulnerabilities that come from living closely to one's neighbor. The vulnerabilities foster a correctional ethos that generates the very categories of unbelonging needed to sustain the threat of the perceived stranger and its spatial disruptions. Trayvon is becoming an architectural subject and object whose unbelongingness elicits a need to stabilize security; Trayvon's mobility, the recognition and negation of him as a stranger, is central to the neighborhood constituting itself as a host and refuge (for some), with capacities to thin out place. In other words, the affinity toward those enclosed within the circuits of the folds uphold settler colonialism's idioms of belonging in and to place; topologically, they are guarded from those perceived to exist outside of the fold's inside. What unfolds in the neighborhood watch is the folding in and out of people, holding-in for the purpose of blocking-out, as though some form of safety can be achieved through this process. This form of the cute—with an outside that is nested in an inside, transforming it from within—accounts for the dizzy temporal dimensions of its many uses.

And yet this acute notion of a cute neighborhood is not protecting twelve-year-old Tamir Elijah Rice, who is being murdered for playing *with* an airsoft pellet gun *on* snow covered grass, *near* a gazebo (that place of rest, a shelter), *in* his neighborhood public park, Cleveland's Cudell Commons, *near* the neighborhood's recreational center (a place of leisure and gathering). This puts him *near* other neighbors, especially given he also lived across the park and spent four to five days a week there, demonstrating the strength of his commitment.[171] That the gazebo, a place of rest, became the place where the police are doing their work of expiring his life shows the squiggly intertwining of leisure and work in such a gathering space. In such a harmony of squiggles, Black leisure is already being perceived as a threat to subdue, puzzling discourse and imagination. A toy gun, in the hands of a Black boy with a demonstrated strength of commitment, becomes an acutely deadly weapon, not a cute object.

Cudell Commons is not a Black commons. Its grounds are harvesting Black life and disregarding Black imagination. Certainly, it is not a place where a Black boy, grounded in the songs of the park, robbed of his relations with the snow-covered grass, is afforded the resources of a neighborhood watch; instead of mutual aid, he is released from the terrain of Cudell Commons. Given his frequent visits, which suggest his hushed embrace of the place, I can imagine the earthly and other-than-earthly lives in the park that transport him into joy, away from the loneliness and isolation of childhood: the birds he's bound to hear and see; the air full of flavors he feels and smells. From his play-walking up and down the sidewalk, creating space in his mind, living as a being in his neighborhood, I can imagine this Black boy dreaming, making and finding folds out of the living world of the park; I imagine him alive, in communion, with the liveliness of Cleveland ash and oak and maple trees.

The neighbor, speaking to the police dispatcher, is seeing the Black child as a "guy [who] keeps pulling [his gun] in and out of his pants. It's probably fake, but you know what, he's scaring the shit out of me."[172] Notwithstanding the caller's recourse to the sexual fantasies of Black masculinity, perception is truly a weapon.

I am using mine to thread some of your befores into a care we denied you.
I am squinting at my screen as if pulling my muscles in and out will exceed my reach for beyond.
In your untimelessness, there's holding.

The neighbor who is reaching for 911, who caught him in a make-believe play with a fake gun in the dead of November, is not seeing the child and his playing as part of a history of cute kids playing a game of cops-and-robbers. The neighbor is not folding this Black boy into the racial aesthetic form of cute and innocent, those sentimental notions of childhood that Robin Bernstein, in *Racial Innocence*, argues, obscures histories and legacies of racial trauma and violence. Crystal Lynn Webster is on point when, meditating on the *longue durée* of violence against Black children in the epilogue to her book *Beyond the Boundaries of Childhood*, she concludes that "the violence considered these boys to be something other than children. By being perceived as deviant, dangerous, or simply adult, these Black children were not only denied their identities as children, but they were also deprived of their lives and humanity."[173]

A cuddle can also deprive us of our living humanity. The space of the neighborhood and its public park and servants do not allow Black boys to be children or have access to childhood. We see how those who have sworn to serve and protect us, whether it is the police or the neighborhood watch, also know how best to dispose of us.

If we move from the microcosm of the neighborhood to the global consumption and display of images of these Black children in the media, we see a different desiring structure of the cuddle-space. The media's engagement with Black children feels like a smothering. In their landmark and controversial essay, "Racist Love," Frank Chin and Jeffery Paul Chan offer insights into the "measure of the success of white racism," which for them is "silence," "and the amount of white energy necessary to maintain or increase that silence."[174] Chin and Chan use the concept of "racist love" to describe the embrace of Asian American men into the social and political folds of white America. Reviewing the significance of this essay, Tara Fickle highlights its "trap of misogyny" by citing King-Kok Cheung's critique: they "buttress patriarchy by invoking gender stereotypes, by disparaging domestic efficiency as feminine, and by slotting desirable traits such as originality, daring, physical courage and creativity under the rubric of masculinity."[175] As Chin and Chan point out, "[e]ach racial stereotype comes in two models—the unacceptable, hostile Black stud has his acceptable counterpart in the form of Stepin Fetchit,"[176] the latter referring to the stage name of the Black comic actor, synonymous with servility. This juxtaposition helps explain the conditions under which the white public offer love, or, in the discourse of this book, cuddle. In death, Black children become acceptable recipients of racist love.

Earlier, I highlighted the clothing in two images that the media circulated of Trayvon Martin: the football jersey and the hooded sweatshirt. I noted how the iconography of each clothing differently positioned our response to him: in one, the "commodity aesthetic"[177] of the all American-football jersey, which acutely obscures the game's underlying aggression, makes us embrace his image (and, by extension, him) as cute, sweet, and innocent. Much has been made of the significance of the hoodie as an object of Blackness and, particularly, Black masculinity. At issue is how a hoodie cradles and stylizes the body of the wearer into visibility at the same time that it offers a cloak of protection by obscuring the face of the wearer. This is to say it is at once about individualizing and collectiviz-ing the wearer, subjecting youths who wear them to risk and danger.

In a 2006 speech at the one-day symposium organized by the Centre of Social Justice, newly elected Conservative party leader and future British Prime minister David Cameron attempted to define his brand of "compassionate conser-vatism" by urging the British nation to see the other sides of "hoodies," here referring to men-acing racialized young men so named for their attire, who, to his mind, do not contribute to the economy.[178] Seeking to present himself as a firm but fair-minded politician, he proclaimed in his speech: "we, the people in suits, see the hoodie as aggressive, the uniform of a rebel army of young gangsters. But, for young people, hoodies are often defensive rather than offensive. They are a way to stay invisible on the street." Subsequently, Cameron's rivals, the sitting Labour Party under PM Tony Blair "used the hug-a-hoodie phrase to make the Tories look cuddly when it came to crime."[179] Cuddly, as understood here, serves as a tool of manipulation. And, as Mimi Thi Nguyen, writing on the hoodie, asks: "What [other] cover, then, does the hoodie provide?"[180]

Implicit in the discussion of the hoodie are strategies of uncuddlification. Consider the ways that the story behind the teddy bear, of fair chase and fugitivity, anticipates the hunting and killing of Trayvon and Tamir. Consider the way these children are being mascotized in the media. Consider the length to which the right-wing media go to make these children and also Michael Brown and so many others, appear uncuddly.

It is with both strategies in mind that I "look squarely into the fucked-up face of things"[181] and ask: what would it mean to turn away *from* the Cudell Commons *to* the Cuddling Undercommons?

There is as much unknown intimacy to be gained in escaping from the cuddlespace of the cuddle commons as there is to be gained in escaping to the cuddle undercommons. As this and the previous chapters show, the cuddlespace is not always a place to escape *to*; as a space that reveals the intimacies of power and violence, it is also a place to escape *from*. The motion in the shadows of *to* and *from* hides the directional motions in the cuddlespace; which is to say, tracing the circuits of desire in the cuddle common reveals how this shadow that accompanies Black life also circumscribes it. So, in this rollercoaster journey, some fold and unfold between unbound bound grooves, others cook, and clean, and shop, and live in other's pocket, desiring limbo.

Hiding in the itinerary of these directional prepositions lies the elusive yet physical spaces in which people who are being made marginalized by power take what they thief. They are stealing away from the existing structures of wealth/power/knowledge to which their labor contributes. It is in these spaces that they are forming the cuddle undercommons. One simply has to think about the coming together of Black (and other) people in the wake of Rice and Martin's death, in the streets, in the vestibules, and how, in these vulnerable architectures, in the vagabond folds/holds, as we grappled with the pain of their deaths, we were also creating a kind of cuddle undercommons we might call intimate fugitivities and we might call fugitive intimacies.

Theater, Hustling, Embrace

In which our author unravels the violent grammar of a
"continuous present" within which Black death through
police cuddling repeats itself in reaction to the ways the
Black market must express itself in the hustle.

In *The Book of Embraces*, Eduardo Galeano notes
that "there is just one place where yesterday and
today meet, recognize each other, and embrace,
and that place is tomorrow."[182] Yesterday and
today have their arms beside tomorrow, mutually
touching and feeling the weight of one another.
And yet yesterday is yesterday and today is today
and tomorrow is tomorrow; they connect because
each causally recognizes a chain through a discon-
nected, dreamy plain. Today and tomorrow are
linked by yesterday in a refiguring of the utopian
and in the recognition of an embrace of the
past/present/future. But none carries the other's
weight. They do, however, attend and even tend to
one another with care. Attending. Tending. Care.

I begin with Galeano's meditation on embrace
as a way to suggest that the cuddle undercommons in which Black people live is operating in the
present continuous. As a verb tense, the present
continuous concerns itself with a relentless proces-
sion of happenings; it communicates any action

or condition that is unfolding *right now*, that occurs *frequently or that is ongoing*. What makes the present continuous of interest to me is that this grammatical tense draws attention to the succession of time (life). The continuous form provides us with a frame within which bumping into an other we have missed, who's also missed, bumping into an other, bringing one other into awareness in time for us to bump into an other, makes the activity of being, to again borrow from Harney and Moten, "incomplete."[183] A common but unique feature of the present continuous has to do with how the present continuously embraces the sensual interactions between the come and go sweep of time going on and on. Keeping this history in the continuity of the present is one key feature of the cuddle undercommons. To live in the present continuous, in the cuddly undercommons, is to live in a way that is not contained by a single now. In the cuddle undercommons, where we see *Black life stretching the grammar* that structures this existential junction, this compositional incompleteness helps me entertain the idea that perhaps *Black life is lived in the present continuous, the continuous present*. After a conversation with a friend about my thinking on the continuous present as it relates to Black life, he sent me a poem, from which I quote:

> Maybe the continuous present is where Black-
> life is always
> emerging, making, creating, enacting itself:
> Brighter Colors,
> Bigger Hair, Bolder Patterns—not drawn by a
> ruler—

improvising soundscapes, styling every move-
    ment, every utterance
Embodying the present continuous:
working the system, the market, the streets,
hustling god's life in the expanding present.[184]

And yet every day, somewhere, a Black person
is mourning the policekilling of another Black
person. This grief is operating in a present continuous, for Black people, the tense of this grief
is right now, frequent, and appears to be ongoing.
I am being drawn to the concept of the continuous form as it indicates that the occurrences are
repetitious and that we are continuing to live in
the racial embrace of a repetitious killing that
is predicated on an economy of difference and
indifference. In the grammar of the present continuous, the repeating embrace is showing an
insistence. I keep wanting to break the laws that
govern the grammar of this tense; I keep wanting
to mark the verb activity of killing of Black men
like Eric Garner and George Floyd to show this
insistence is incomplete; their untimely deaths
continue to ricochet in the public imagination
with various implications. The dominant script,
the hegemonic choreography, is insisting we place
the policekillings in the embrace of the tense past.
But remember what Dionne Brand says about
history? That it "is already seated in the chair in
the empty room when one arrives. Where one
stands in a society seems always related to this historical experience. Where one can be observed is
relative to that history."[185]

What has all of this to do with cuddling? In this state of continuous present where death is continuing to chip away at Black life, premature death's ongoing presence is elongating the present so that it shapes in the continuity of the past and the future. Being present in a continuous present is akin to how a cuddling composition of bodies embraces a prolonged present: being is not fixed to presence or absence. There is no middle in the passage of cuddling. It opens moments of cuddling life backward and forward and sideways. It extends from Emmett Till into the present, to Eric Garner and George Floyd. Which is to say, that continuity is shaping the verb of the moment.

On July 18, 2014, I woke up to messages from friends. I soon learned their messages of care were in response to a video of Eric Garner being murdered by the hands of the New York City police. The public performance of police brutality is not news to many Black men; what the recording of the footage is displaying is the police's unfiltered relationship to touch and their wholesale use of force in the pursuit of arrest. The clip begins with two police officers approaching Eric Garner, accusing him of pursuing the selling of illegal cigarettes. We hear Mr. Garner responding with "I ain't selling nothing." We are seeing the officers mobilizing the one-talks-one-tackles technique as they are trying to arrest him, grabbing at him, attempting a take down. Eric Garner is pulling away from their hands as a way to pull away from the officers. Officer Daniel Pantaleo is grabbing Garner by his neck and they are both falling forward onto the sidewalk, breaking a store window. We are seeing all four officers grabbing at the fallen man, holding him down. The officers are placing Eric Garner in a prone position; one is handcuffing him, and, for a few seconds, we are seeing another officer restraining Garner by putting his arm around his neck. He releases only when Garner has finished saying "I can't breathe" eleven times. Emergency vehicles are arriving; however, they do not have oxygen. Eric Garner was pronounced dead on the way to the hospital.

Again; on Monday, May 25, 2020, and its ensuing days, my phone beeped and rang with a frequency that made me switch its audible announcement of an incoming message to a vibratory one. I did because, in the midst of a global health pandemic, when forms of living are forced into a digital migratory journey, I needed sound relief; the stress of social isolation, of trying to avoid infection as a result of immunocompromised system and living alone, made me miss physical contact, and the repeated vibrations, that week, became a way for me to feel the touch of those reaching for me. They were concerned because another Black man has been cuddled to death by those who have sworn to serve and protect him. This theater of deadly cuddling is taking place in the city of Minneapolis, where the hip-hop artist George Floyd is going into a family-owned grocery store to buy cigarettes. There, a 17-year-old clerk believing that George Floyd is buying his cigarettes with a counterfeit 20-dollar bill, begins calling the police. Four Minneapolis police officers are arriving to arrest this 46-year-old Black father. Seventeen minutes later, he is dying. One of the officers is pinning Floyd to the ground, on a roadside in Minneapolis. He is pressing his knee into Floyd's neck for more than eight minutes and 46 seconds, squeezing the breath and life out of him. The world, watching, sees a Minneapolis police officer murdering George Floyd, while two other officers are assisting by holding his body down. Another is keeping the crowd away. A young Black bystander is pleading with the police to release Floyd as she is filming the gruesome display with her cellphone.

The continuous present in which such actions are continuing to transpire is built around a form of racial capitalism that, as we have seen, takes different historical approaches to the problem and solution of Black labor. Yet its dominant chronotope would erase the continuous present and its violence with narratives of progress, where the spreading benefits of capitalism and opportunities for entrepreneurship will gradually release us from the hold of prejudice and the necessity of criminal activity.

In *On Property*, Rinaldo Walcott explores the ways that the carceral state is, under racial capitalism, a "central node of economic activity" and it uses the "logic of law and order" to organize itself around the defense of private property.[186] Having emerged from a process where people were transformed into property, Black people are, he writes, always at odds with that system. As such, "crime tends to find Black people; or to put it another way, the police find Black people and, in doing so, find crime." He doesn't stop there. Thinking through the criminal tactics of police profiling, he argues that "what constitutes crime, and how criminality is assessed by those 'trained' to find it, is most often centered on Black people."[187]

In the prose of poses that strangle Black lives, a tell breaks through in these two videos: the police officers are muscling in on Garner and Floyd just when these two Black men are feared to be exercising their fugitive ingenuity as economic subjects, just when they are appearing to refuse a mode of evaluation that renders them vulnerable in/to the market economy. These policekillings are happening on the economic stage.

Much has been made of Mr. Garner and Mr. Floyd's physical size. In the wake of his killing, we learned that George Floyd's friends and family called him "Big Floyd" and "Gentle Giant." Eric Garner weighed over 350 pounds, almost double the mass of the police officer who choked him, though the latter was given heft by institutional power of the repressive state.

Their large size and cuddly physique are adding a melodramatic element to their slaying. The physical theatricality in these poses depicts a history of political economy and policing that can be traced back to the melodrama of nineteenth-century novels and theater, specifically the theatricality of the market's instability and the drama of masculine control. By referring to melodrama I am not conflating the grim facts of life and death with the cheap generic devices used by Hollywood and other commercial cultural industries to shape tantalizingly implausible plots and exaggerated conflicts. Broadly and historically speaking, melodrama's gift is that it works to ensure that readers and viewers do not miss the knowledge embedded in the magnetic spectacle of plots and conflicts. As a genre, it can make the suffering of marginalized life-forms legible. The brutal intensity of violence in the videos of the policekillings of Garner and Floyd make melodrama a valuable frame within which to imagine the sublime processes that go into choreographing the fatal embrace of these hustling men. The theatricality in the poses depict the deteriorating consequences that the economic drive of the market has on the masculinity of Black men and their bodies. I was also thinking of how Garner and Floyd performed themselves as economic disobedient subjects in or on the black market. Because an economic life is enmeshed in a poetics of place and time, the narrative drama that surrounds the work Garner and Floyd did to make ends meet has a lot to teach us about how markets are embedded in social practices and institutional arrangements of racial capitalism.

In his famous autobiography, Malcolm X tells of his education as an entrepreneurial hustler on the black market, and throughout his life he would often mobilize this knowledge to critique white capitalism's unpunished crimes and contextualize the criminalization of black people's acts of economic survival. The clean separation between legitimate commerce and the black market is belied by the history of the transatlantic slave trade, where practices now associated with both were refined. The slave trade, therefore, is a black market bent on making illegal transactions legal, and, in this market, encoding Blackness and Black people as cultural and moral transgressors.

In a capitalist economy built on slavery, claims to any kind of "logic" in the system are bogus. We can see that the fact that these men are being murdered in retribution for extremely minor economic "crimes" defies capitalism's claims to economic rationality, let alone economic freedom; therefore, we must necessarily see these deadly theaters of cuddling as forms of white supremacist theater where "the economy" is the stage set for choreographing Black death.

And if, from one (important) angle, "the economy" is only a stage on which the tragedy and melodrama unfold in a continuous present, one thing we cannot lose sight of is that hustling is a gerund: a verb transmuted into a noun, where the action is locked in place, as in "Garner and Floyd's *killing* is a response to the way their *hustling* is being criminalized"; nor can we afford losing sight of the fact that the hustler knows they don't have access to the official system of the market; hustling, then, is a performing-out of a continuous—long experienced—present. It is intentional and its dynamics are a containing of hope. Hope is hustling for today. The hoping of the hustler insists that I can and I will.

According to Sara Ahmed's *Willful Subjects*, the police legitimate themselves as an expression of the "general will" that is fading into the background, and against which the (deviant) willful subject appears. For her, "to be identified as willful is to become a problem."[188] "Willfulness," Ahmed goes on to point out, "is a diagnosis of the failure to comply with those whose authority is given"; for her, "willfulness involves persistence in the face of having been brought down."[189] Eric Garner is becoming a problem not simply because he is refusing arrest for being part of the street capital of his neighborhood; also, he is a problem because, as we learn from Matt Taibbi in *I Can't Breathe: A Killing on Bay Street*, the theater of the neighborhood is changing. A new billion-dollar real estate development and a row of condominium towers are sprouting up. A businessman like Mr. Garner, a big slovenly-dressed man, constantly sick with a runny nose so that he wiped with his hand on his pants, was attracting police attention. As Taibbi explains, the police were stopping people whose appearance contradicted the changing neighborhood.[190] This policing of Black poverty recalls Stuart Hall's argument that "race is the *modality* in which class is lived, the *medium* through which class relations are experienced, the *form* in which it is appropriated and fought through."[191]

Much is being made of the chokehold, and on whether or not the technique of restraint being used to murder Mr. Garner was in fact one. We know from the report the officers filed on the confrontation that they did not mention its use. Others have challenged that a distinction must be drawn between a chokehold and a lateral vascular neck restraint. The former places pressure on the front of the neck to decrease a target's ability to breathe or to cut off their air supply; the latter is a technique where one part of an officer's arm, the forearm, embraces one side of the neck, where the coronary artery lies; the other part of their arm, the upper part, the biceps, covers the target's other artery; you pinch the sides of the neck, not the front, restricting blood flow to the brain, making the target lose consciousness: the body is talking to the mind, the body is pushing pause, taking a break, a timeout. It is this latter technique that is taking Garner's life.

Recall the two etymological roots of cuddle: *coler*, from the Old French, meaning "neck, collar"; *collare*, from the Latin, meaning "necklace, band or chain for the neck." Recall that the second meaning is connected to an early sixteenth-century use of the word *cull* or *coll*, meaning "to embrace." This embrace, in the sixteenth century, is linked to collar, which can mean both "to grab by the neck" and "to capture" (typically, a fugitive). These origins foreground cuddling as an embrace of the neck. Hence, whether the technique being used to kill Eric Garner is a banned technique of a chokehold or the controlled technique of a lateral vascular neck restraint, both involve an "embrace" of his neck, a state-sponsored cuddling meant to restrain his lifeline, to time out his life.

Eric Garner is being held, cuddled, for the selling of contraband cigarettes on the black market, for being the wrong kind of economic subject. Garner is found a criminal for operating within an underground economy, one that is working against the economic and structural constraints that embrace him. He is making that structural situation work to his benefit, making him the wrong kind of entrepreneur for the state.

I cannot help but connect this scene of Black entrepreneurship to George Floyd, who is also being murdered because of his presumed criminalized interactions with the economy. Both men in some ways are breaching the norms and conventions of the white market and are being executed for it through this murderous cuddling. And yet, ironically, under racial capitalism, Black and white capitalists are responding to the aftermath of the murders with plenty of opportunities for legitimate Black mentorship in the form of entrepreneurship programs, role models, education/business loans.

At each turn that Black people enter the market, even on their own terms, it becomes a moment of their possible death. From the market's viewpoint, avoiding taxes for the cigarettes and circulating counterfeit money justify the men's death. Tax avoidance and counterfeit are both counter to the official market. But clearly, these actions are both regularly performed by the market (tax avoidance as a way to get richer) and state (monetary creation for national debt, for example).

It's Almost Time

for the tulips.
It means I've survived springtime
death though we all know
they'll link
my flowering to the silky murmur
of white grass.

How many times must I hear the jays squirrel
the noise-infested sky,
the worms nip on my roots
before I matter?

Behold o! An early morning stroller
reaches out.
Whispers to his lover, it is
almost time for the tulips. I receive this cargo,
we wait on each other as new
lovers do,

        then fold it away.

Fugitive
(Solidarity (Betrayals))

*In which our author meditates on the spaces of resistance
and autonomy within, against and beyond the racial
embrace while warning us of the lures of solidarity and
the persistence of betrayal.*

The unknowingness that informed the beginning of this book continues to sway me. And so,
as we conclude, I have not sought after the clarity
and poise of closures. That is to say, I don't hold
the conclusive answers that would satisfy many
readers, or myself, nor am I interested in such
satisfaction. This book's cohabitation with cuddling has demonstrated that my interests lie in the
generative nodes that animate practices and processes of thinking and the way these can reveal the
complex ecologies of togetherness; I am drawn to
the sense-feeling-thinking practices and processes
that unfold the accumulated mass/mess we are
given.

Thinking with cuddling during the twin pan-
demics of Covid-19 and anti-Black violence of
police brutality has been rewardingly painful. My
embodied practice of writing about Black vulnerabilities as I lived in the continuous present of

such violence was a strange labor. My heart broke, and broke again.

Triangulating the era of Covid-19, the movements for Black lives, and the heightening climate crisis, there has also been a strange labor of loneliness that accompanied repositioning myself, again and again, to ready myself for the given task, for the difficulty of bracketing one political fervor from the other. Such bracketing is especially vexing when we find ourselves embraced by institutions hungry for anti-colonial, anti-capitalist, and decolonial rhetorics, though rarely in good faith. This strange labor has me grappling the quiet uncertain wait of restlessness; reposing in bed over dreams tearing air from hair so I can recompose scattered and unheard selves; surviving for an other and another, alone, an unalone I, fluent in waiting, going nowhere, did not know, truly not know of cuddling's love to the point of death. Those of us who enjoy an embarrassment of love in the hands of institutions, eventually we come to know such love can kill you. Many of us are being loved to our death in these grips, love's labor in us a heavy burden which we carry and shoulder, tripping on every you, busy busy turning from one another and open spaces.

I have learned to think twice about solidarity. I am not bracketing off how the strange labor of this moment also includes envisioning ways of creating connections and building new bonds; rather, I want to disabuse myself of relishing comfortable thoughts about concepts and practices such as creation, community, and solidarity, especially given how each of these concepts and practices bespeak uneven labor and struggle with diverse consequences. When we take solidarity to mean laboring in struggle together, and remember how practices of solidarity are based on material and imagined senses of community, our sense of what constitutes the political community becomes capacious and historically-minded. This less celebratory image of solidarity is a relational acknowledgment of our responsibility toward an other, which includes one's self; solidarity becomes a practice of neighboring, fur and hide. It is less a performative presence of living side-by-side and more an ethics of presencing, within which we develop the capacity to grow together, differently. We develop a capacity to grow with and in difference, not in opposition.

The word *bracketing*, I will admit, gestures a shift from grammar to punctuation. As an architectural metaphor, the perceptual-cum-visual frame of the bracket, which resembles an enclosure, is my attempt to cuddle the concept of communities with the care of parenthesis. And yet, this home, this nest, as I've been showing with the cuddlespace, can also be a space for state cuddling and Black vulnerabilities. And so this detour, of huddling in-between the brackets, impels an epistemological reflection on the everyday, banal practices that sustain us, demonstrating that cuddling is a manipulable form of relationality. The tender arm of a lover, holding you, can easily echo (or be haunted by) the long arm of the state, holding and disciplining you. This knowing is not my attempt to deny or foreclose the transformative, life sustaining potentials in cuddling. But . . .

The cuddle, the embrace, the hug are all symbols of community care. To bring the nourishing work that the hug and the embrace and the cuddle accomplish, let us remember values in the temporality of a hug and those in the temporality of a cuddle and ask how each of these helps us understand not only the question of home, with which I began, but also meditate on the poetic work required to create communities and build solidarity. How, for example, the pressing of borders in a hug has a lot to teach us about the borders we press against within communities. How, for example, a hug can remind us that home is never permanent or secure. Irrespective of the accumulated mess that brackets cuddling, I hold great desires for the hell of sweat that puddles the parentheses, the home we make in the cuddle: its long duration can offer time off for regeneration and replenishment from all sorts of exhaustions, including bodily. This desire to ride the crescent light of two little moons and meditate on the partnership between the open parenthesis and the closed parenthesis leads us not only to find rest in the nesting space in between, nor only to feel for the pressures that press against the outside and inside boundaries of the moons. My turn to these syntactical marks (typically used to mark an aside or afterthought) is my way of saying I am as interested in making poetry out of cuddling as I am in thinking through the additional yet inaudible information that nestles in the deep bowl of a community's caring embrace. As the dynamics of this book demonstrate, the poems assembled insist on their non-linear politics at the same time that the politics is connected to the poetry (even if the totality of the connections is indeterminable, tenuous, and not always graspable by you, by any one person).

Etymologically, parenthesis means literally "put in beside" (from the Greek *para-*, meaning "beside, near" whence the Latin, "alongside," and from the Latin *-en from which English derives the preposition* "in.") My interest in the parenthesis, then, recalls the prepositional life of Blackness: at once part and also separate from the action of the text, demonstrating the ontological plurality of a sentence. Earlier, when I mentioned writing this book in the continuous present of Black death, I was writing in parenthesis (it was an insertion in need of separation or protection from public sentences, I was not set apart from the stream of public sentences, I was inviting readers to think about the simultaneous happenings). Which is to say, in the parenthetical world of Black life, lives effaced (those parenthesized, kept in the hold, under eyes, on the run, and over policed) take over the sentence (grammatical). The parenthetical walls at once delineate (offering a structure for secret and delicate exchanges) and suspend narrative progression, and, in so doing, maximize the cuddlespace of intimacy. The parenthetical expression brackets a thought away from its larger context; and it always depends for its meaningfulness on that larger context; it is a form of improvisational meaning-making.

The crescent shape of the parenthesis (celestial) conjures up the wave of a tide upon the rotating earth (terrestrial), flooding my imagination with stormy images of waves, of sea change, folding and cuddling the earth. The architecture of the tides recalls the tidal waves we feel in cuddling, but there's more. Newton's first law of motion (there must be a cause—however ungraspable—for there to be any change in velocity) should lead us to recognize that there is much to learn from the gravity exercised on the movement of tides by the moon in its phases relative to the position of the earth rotating around the sun.[192] We know the gravitational forces of the moon and sun cause the oceans to rise and fall, and that this tidal ebb and flow also shapes the bulge of the waves, which changes the shape of the fold, changing the tidal cuddle. My interest in the tides is less mechanical and more phenomenological (the symphonic strategies afforded in knowing that the state of the tides can save lives). Knowing that tides are local phenomena, what methods will help each of us navigate and refuse the racial embrace?

Kamau Brathwaite uses the tidal procedures of the sea to assert the rhythmic continuum of Caribbean life and history. In *ConVERSations with Nathaniel Mackey*, we get his political riddle of "tidalectics" which moonlights as a fugitive theory that diffuses the chrononormativity of the dialectical tension.[193] (I invoke Elizabeth Freeman's idea of chrononormativity because the instituted way of regulating time is also an apparatus for state cuddling). For Brathwaite, "dialectics is another gun: a missile: a way of making progress: / farward /."[194] His precise meaning of dialectic is to be debated; more so if we heed Curdella Forbes' argument of the "paradox" that constitutes Caribbean poetics, literature, and theory.[195] And yet, if we read the revolutionary spirit in tidalectics and consider it a revolutionary weapon that allowed anti-colonial thinkers to mobilize community,[196] then it is possible that Brathwaite strategically mobilized dialectics to deal with the primary contradiction in the discourse of his time, knowing its limitations, thus allowing us to experience it through the politics of their writing.

Rejecting this successful fate of dialectics, under the banner of "synthesis," Brathwaite is interested in the kinds of success that "moves outward from the center to circumference and back again: a tidal dialectic: an ital dialectic: continuum across peristyle,"[197] emphasizing the livity, the life-force in continuous emergence, imprecision, and non-linear lives, histories, and futures. Tidalectics, for him, is "dialectics with *my* difference."[198] We cannot overlook that this quotation is from an essay that examines the paradigm that Western history uses to measure revolution, and how, in surveying the change and flux that revolutionary moments entail, he asserts/inserts upon his difference. "[I]nstead of the notion of one-two-three Hegelian," he continues, "I am now more interested in the movement of the water backwards and forwards as a kind of cyclic, I suppose, motion, rather than linear."[199] In contrast to what we have been led to expect from Newtonian laws that value predictability, tidalectics teaches us that, within the geography and ecology of this infinite set of motions, we might find an interplay of practices, structures, and belief systems that revise themselves to assert hope, hope through traditions of the imagination. Brathwaite suggests that our psychology

> is not dialectical—successfully dialectical—in the way that Western philosophy has assumed people's lives should be, but tidalectic like our grandmother's—our nanna's—actions, like the movement of the ocean she's walking on, coming from one continent/continuum, touching another, and then receding (reading) from the island(s) into the perhaps creative chaos of the(ir) future."[200]

There are gravitational interactions mediating this saturated choreography of Caribbean psychology. That "our psychology is tidalectic" dispels the "nauseating mimicry" born out of what Fanon sees as an economic and internalized inferiority complex;[201] in other words, it dispels easily definable perceptions of Blackness, perceptions that perpetuate epistemic violence that ignores the culture, history, and psyche of colonization, slavery, displacement of peoples, and of genocide, perceptions that do not adhere to the complex system of family dynamics that undergird Black culture, and those that overlook the embodiment of joy in being Black. In his repudiation, Brathwaite repositions our lives within practices without closures, practices that resist pinning down our lives. In the undercurrents of the sea's advance-retreat choreography, in this continuous return that does not endorse the continuous present, acts of creative chaos help us evade capture. Simply think of how tides repeat themselves predictably, and how they actually wear away the present: their wax and wane actually changes, resculpts, the landscapes that physically embrace their waters. When placed in relation to the weather of racial politics, these repetitive cycles do not account a narrative of despair (a depressing cycle of violence, suppression, and liberation). Rather, the tides' iteration (predictable, repeated action of tides) and change (how the land that brackets the oceans is resculpted by the tides), is not exactly synthesis (as conveyed in the two opposing forces of dialectics); the changes generated by tides are "beside the point." The forces of moon gravity and earth gravity that move water do their work on something else (shorelines and such). In this way, there is an action of permanent change in tidalectics; the borders of racial embrace are changing, and, as tides wear away at lands that embraces them, we note ways the physical cartography of where you are is being eroded, too. Their incessant imprecisions and irregularities teach us how to disrupt the undertow of the racial embrace.

Keeping in mind the idea of parenthesis as tidalectics, as a structure for intimacy and privacy, for disruption and interruption (and, like tides to slavery and indentureship in the Islands, what they hide are not always a structure of protection, they are dangerous and can kill you), let me return to my attempt to cuddle the concept of communities. I want to return with the care of parenthesis, and to use what lies inside and outside the parenthetical structure to think through what lies outside (public narrative) and inside (intimate private exchanges) the dynamics of belonging in a community and being entitled to its care.

Elsewhere I have thought about community care and used the example of the academic context to think about fugitive solidarity.[202] There, I read American slave narratives as archives of both solidarity and of betrayal. I argued that "the threats of betrayal are not isolated to the history of fugitives. The history of solidarity has its own archives of betrayals. Such stories of intimate betrayal, however, are not the full story within the archives of fugitive solidarity." Then I argued that fugitive communities "were aware of the racial violence of betrayal. Fugitives even sometimes betrayed one another." I prophesied that none of us are "immune to solidarity and betrayal's dialectical relationship." I believed that the transformative aspects of fugitive solidarity are "marked by our coming to terms with the competing entangled histories and interests that condition our lives"; I went so far as to say that "one way for fugitive solidarity to deal with the promise of betrayal, politically, is to understand that imagination is more valuable than knowledge."

As forms of exchange with sets of parameters, the parentheses that embrace betrayal and solidarity open and close infinitely. If we recall the betrayal of the state's promise of solidarity, then the cuddle undercommons is possible because of an awareness that the dialectic of solidarity and betrayal can turn into a tidalectic, unfolding an advance-retreat choreography between the two, reshaping the fabric of living to show how solidarity and betrayal work hand in hand with community.

Here, perhaps, lies a form of creative chaos: the generativity that Brand, describing Jazz, regards as "an opening to another life tangled up in this one but opening." Whether stylized or not, there is a form of creative potency in chaos. Simply think of the chaos in the funk imaginary, of how Black narrative around Black art exhibits a creative chaos. Chaos, then, brings a new form into being. Here I think of Cornelius Castoriadis who tells us that great art "is the unveiling of chaos through a giving form" (note the gerund) and that "giving form is the creation of a cosmos."[203] I have used cuddling for the giving of creative form to the chaotic violence of state cuddling. The parenthesis of cuddling, which I hope conveys the weight of Black vulnerability, becomes a creation that shows how the larger world creates a world that kills Black life. Now, what do we do with this temporary but repeated opening? How do we create a world that refuses the world that wants us dead?

VĀG
ABO
NDS

Acknowledgments

The weight of my gratitude is testimony to the fact that I've cuddled, been cuddled, and will cuddle so many more that I haven't yet met.

I am overwhelmed by the debts that I incurred while becoming the person who finished this book. So, if cuddling is a fleshy mode of storytelling, then this acknowledgment archives intimacies, and these intimacies contain an archive of debt. While not many intimacies can be properly named, many debts can, and, below, I've tried to archive some of the debts that made this book possible.

To Max Haiven, my editor and friend, whose talent for the weird shepherded this book into the incarnation you're holding in your hand. Thank you profusely for your belief in this project from day one: without you this book would not be here.

To all the team at Pluto Press, my heartfelt gratitude for your patience and diligence, especially to Emily Orford, David Shulman, and Robert Webb.

To all the artists and writers whose work I cite—thank you for offering ideas to cuddle with.

To Curdella Forbes and Faith Smith: thank you for your brilliant and generous readings. Your feedback and suggestions not only assured me there's a project here worth fine tuning but also you offered language that inched me closer to understanding this work. I remain happily in your debt.

To Michael Bucknor, Daniel Coleman, Wendy Coleman, Amber Dean, and Jade Ferguson: you've held me in ways I never expected I would need. Thank you for giving me your faith when mine disappeared. I will return your faith one of these days. I feel blessed and nourished by your care.

To Steve Dadds, Benjamin Hilb, and Ian Williams: your willingness to engage in the experiment of thinking fills me with wonder. Your companionships from the beginning of this project are on every page. Thanks for them conversations.

To Nadine Attewell and Sarah Tremble: in its molten stage, you were this book's first readers. I am humbled by your incisive feedback. Your questions make thinking possible.

To Lesley Loksi Chan: in so many ways, without your companionship none of this is possible. Not only are you kind, unbelievably generous, funny and smart in equal measures, you also beam these qualities onto me and for that thank you.

To Lyndon Kamal Gill: thanks for showing up when you did, all those years ago, at the AGO, cajoling me to dance with ideas in paintings. I'm looking forward to further dancing with you.

To Jorge Amigo, Adam Davidson, Aldrich Leung, Tasha Nijjar, Zian Sally, and Shireen Soofi: for ongoing support and solidarity and for making the pandemic livable.

To Y-Dang Troung, Christopher Patterson, Kai, Danielle Wong, David Chariandy, Sophie McCall, Skye Chariandy, Maya Chariandy, Christine Kim, Yusef Varachia, Zahra and Zidan: thanks for creating a space that made Vancouver feel a little more hospitable.

To The Negro Field Collective (Sara Ghebremusse, Darryl Dijon, and Rohene Bouajram): we done things. We doing things. We gon do things. You each inspire wonder and joy. Long live this luminous love for life.

To Denise Ferreira Da Silva and Mark Harris: this way of living experimentally will forever be my way through guide. I can't thank you enough.

To Ronald Cummings and Nalini Mohabir: the intellectual and political journeys from Leeds to Toronto to Montreal have buoyed me over the years. Thank you.

To the organizers who supported the ideas in this book by inviting me to engage in dialogue, thank you: the F-Word Conference organizers (2015); Sean Kennedy, convener of the Queering Ireland conference (2015); and Thy Phu for convening the Visualities and Racial Capitalism panel at ASA (2019). Presenting work in progress at each of these gatherings helped pivot my thinking in unexpected ways.

To my boyz: Alowen Browne, Mike Baichoo, Kareem Bunyan, and Christopher Browne; Rayon Browne and Dipo Togonu-Bickersteth; John de Flon and Greg Shreeves; Derrick Chang, Jordan Huntington, Jonathan Odumeru, and Robin Morden—your boy wrote a book. A lot here comes from conversations from driving and walking the streets of Rexdale, Toronto, and Guelph, and Hamilton, and Wolverhampton, and Stockholm; from holding ourselves alongside each other as we lapse into and out of flows; from failing to know how to be there for one another. In your different ways, you each wedged open doors, cajoled me to enter doors when I was too shy, and encouraged me to keep at life when the keeping got tough. I am growing still, and our days carry me through.

To the Girlfriends: Angela Ampadu, Eli Bamfo, Tina Mena, and Natacha Pennycooke, thanks for the invitation and the lifeline. I remain lucky for that fateful encounter in McKinnon building, when Angie and Eli chased me down with a script. Almost 20 years later, the characters have grown, and we continue to script new lives, and each is so damn beautiful.

To The Espiritus (Karen, Kristine, Mede, Fernando, and Marlow): Fragment Boy turned some of those fragments into sentences. I remain fragmenty. I remember everything: thank you.

To Leigh Claire La Berge and John Munro: We began at Saint Mary's University, and I'm grateful for the ways we've learned to begin again in different parts of the world. Thanks for the writing workshop in Berlin: you helped renew my belief in the power of attention.

To the roll call of people I have been lucky to have conversations with all these years. Your generous insights have taught me so much. Andrea Actis, Rolando Aguilera, Hari Alluri, Rodrigo Munoz Arana, Stephen Arogundade, Wes Attewell, Andrew Bateman, Octavia Bright, Sarah Brophy, Julie Okot Bitek, Jenn Blair, Darby Minott Bradford, John Brennan, Nanok Cha, Sara Sejin Chang, Scott Clarke, Glen Coulthard, Tim Crabtree, Tanya Davis, Junie Desil, Hannah Dyer, Mercedes Eng, Elisa Ferrari, Jon Fiddler, Jessie Forsyth, Rawi Hage, Chris Harris, Teresa Heffernan, Omaar Hena, Dehlia Hannah, Kit Holden, Jenn Jackson, Ben Evans James, Asha Jeffers, Val Marie Johnson, Cory Legassic, Jason Lem, Joanne Leow, Nilani Loganathan, Terence Lowe, Johnny Mack, Greg Mackie, Jacqueline Maloney, Evan Mauro, Casey Mecija, Sehtareh Mohammadi, Maral Moradipour, Dory Nason, Vin Nardizzi, Ryan Newell, Cecily Nicholson, Anton Nimblett, Naki Osutei, Byron Peters, M. NourbeSe Philip, Denise Ryner, Alia Said, Connie Saieva, Aaron Shaughnessy, Robin Simpson, Naava Smolash, Anakana Schofield, Madeleine Thien, Cassie Thornton, Jennifer VanderBurg, Asha Varadharajan, Karina Vernon, Christian Vistan, Riisa Walden, Dagmawi Woubshet, shō yamagushiku, Jamie Yard, AND many, many more.

To my family, near and far, your unwavering love sustains me.

VĀG
ABO
NDS

Notes

1. Sara Ahmed, *On Being Included: Racism and Diversity in Institutional Life* (Durham: Duke University Press, 2012).

2. Phanuel Antwi and Ronald Cummings, "1865 and the Disenchantment of Empire," *Cultural Dynamics* 31, no. 3 (2019): 167.

3. See, as example, Amy Muise and her colleagues' study on how spooning, after sex, promotes sexual and relationship satisfaction. "Better Sex Life, Closer Relationship Results from More Post-Coital Cuddling, Canadian study suggests," *National Post*, http://life.nationalpost.com/2014/05/28/better-sex-life-closer-relationships-result-from-more-post-coital-cuddling-canadian-study-suggests.

4. Jacque Derrida, *Of Grammatology* (Baltimore: The Johns Hopkins University Press, 1997), p. 46.

5. Christine Miserandino, "The Spoon Theory," *But You Don't Look Sick*, https://butyoudontlooksick.com/articles/written-by-christine/the-spoon-theory [accessed 11 August 2021].

6. Avery Gordon, *Ghostly Matters: Haunting and the Sociological Imagination* (Minneapolis: University of Minnesota Press, 2008), p. 4.

7. Laurent Berlant, "Intimacy: Special Issue," *Critical Inquiry* 24, no. 2 (Winter 1998): 281.

8. Nel Noddings, *Caring: A Feminine Approach to Ethics and Moral Education* (Berkeley, CA: University of California Press, 1984), p. 28.

9. Fred Moten, *In the Break: The Aesthetics of the Black Radical Tradition* (Minneapolis: Minnesota Press, 2003).

10. Saidiya Hartman, *Scenes of Subjection: Terror, Slavery, and Self-Making in Nineteenth-Century America* (Oxford: Oxford University Press, 1997), p. 4.

11. Ranging from sexual abuse to domestic violence.

12. Stefano Harney and Fred Moten speak of "the experiment of the hold" in *The Undercommons: Fugitive Planning and Black Study* (Brooklyn: Autonomedia, 2013), p. 99.

13. Denise Ferreira da Silva, *Unpayable Debt* (London: Sternberg Press, 2022).

14. Paul Gilroy, *The Black Atlantic: Modernity and Double Consciousness* (Cambridge, MA: Harvard University Press, 1993), p. 190.

15. Homi Bhabha, *The Location of Culture* (London: Routledge, 1994), p. 256.

16. Ibid., p. 5.

17. Jean-Luc Nancy, *Being Singular Plural,* translated by Robert D. Richardson and Anne E. O'Byrne (Redwood City: Stanford University Press, 2000), p. 3.

18. Tim Dean, *Unlimited Intimacy: Reflections on the Subculture of Bearbacking* (Chicago: University of Chicago Press, 2009).

19. Orlando Patterson, *Slavery and Social Death: A Comparative Study* (Cambridge, MA: Harvard University Press, 1982), p. 60.

20. Ann Laura Stoler, "Tense and Tender Ties: The Politics of Comparison in North American History and (Post)-Colonial

Studies," in *Haunted by Empire: Geographies of Intimacy in North American History* (Durham, NC: Duke University Press, 2006), p. 13.

21. Judith Butler, *Precarious Life: The Powers of Mourning and Violence* (London and New York: Verso, 2006), p. 33.

22. Sylvia Wynter, "1492: A New World View," in *Race, Discourse, and the Origin of the Americas: A New World View*, eds., Sylvia Wynter, Vera Lawrence Hyatt, and Rex (Nettleford: Smithsonian Institution Press, 1995), pp. 5–57.

23. Sylvia Wynter, "Unsettling the Coloniality of Being/Power/Truth/Freedom: Towards the Human, After Man, It's Overrepresentation— An Argument," *CR: The New Centennial Review* 3, no. 3 (2003): 268.

24. Wynter, "1492."

25. Ash Amin, "Lively Infrastructure," *Theory, Culture and Society* 31, no. 7–8 (December 1, 2014): 137–61; Michelle Murphy, *The Econominzation of Life* (Durham, NC: Duke University Press, 2017); Gabriel Rosenberg, "Sings of the State," in *The 4-H Harvest: Sexuality and the State in Rural America* (Philadelphia: UP Press, 2015), pp. 1–20; AbdouMaliq Simone, "People as Infrastructure: Intersections in Johannesburg," *Public Culture* 16, no. 3 (Fall 2004): 407–29.

26. Tyron P. Woods, "Putting Afro-Pessimism, Intersectionality, and Solidarity to Work," *Black Agenda Report: News, Commentary and Analysis from the Black Left*, 2018. https://blackagendareport.com/putting-afro-pessimism-intersectionality-and-solidarity-work [accessed December 2022].

27. Christina Sharpe, *Monstrous Intimacies: Making Post-Slavery Subjects* (Durham, NC: Duke University Press, 2010), p. 12.

28. From the logic of the Fugitive Slave Law of 1793.

29. Rinaldo Walcott, *On Property: Policing, Prisons, and the Call for Abolition* (Windsor, ON: Biblioasis, 2021).

30. *Liberator*, October 18, 1850.

31. Quoted in Natheniel Mackey, *Discrepant Engagement: Dissonance, Cross-Culturality and Experimental Writing* (Cambridge, UK: Cambridge University Press, 1993), p. 200.

32. Saidiya Hartman, *Wayward Lives, Beautiful Experiments: Intimate Histories of Riotous Black Girls, Troublesome Women, and Queer Radicals* (New York: W. W. Norton & Company, 2019), p. 19.

33. Fred Moten, "Notes on Passage (The New International of Soveryn Feelings)" *Palimpsest: A Journal on Women, Gender, and the Black International* 3, no. 1 (2014): 51–74.

34. Much like how Heidegger reads the jug: the thingness of the jug is not material but the way it shapes the void.

35. Adam Hochschild, *Bury the Chains: Prophets and Rebels in the Fight to Free an Empire's Slaves* (Boston, MA: Mariner Books, 2006).

36. Dorothy Roberts, *Killing the Black Body: Race, Reproduction, and the Meaning of Liberty* (New York: Vintage Books, 1997).

37. Walter Benjamin, *The Arcades Project*, ed., Rolf Tiedemann, trans. Howard Eiland and Kevin McLaughlin (Cambridge, MA: Belknap Press of Harvard University Press, 1999), p. 171.

38. Brian Lavery, *The Arming and Fitting of English Ships of War, 1600–1815* (Annapolis: US Naval Institute Press, 1988), p. 192.

39. Stephanie Smallwood, *Saltwater Slavery: A Middle Passage from Africa to American Diaspora* (Cambridge, MA: Harvard University Press, 2007), p. 101.

40. Marcus Rediker, *The Slave Ship: A Human History* (London: Penguin Books, 2007); Saidiya Hartman, *Lose Your Mother: A Journey Along the Atlantic Slave Route* (New York: Farrar, Straus and Giroux, 2007); Simone Browne, *Dark Matters: On the Surveillance of Blackness* (Durham, NC: Duke University Press, 2015).

41. Wilson Harris, "History, Fable and Myth in the Caribbean and Guianas," in *Selected Essays of Wilson Harris: The Unfinished Genesis of the Imagination* (London and New York: Routledge, 2005), p. 159.

42. John Keegan, *The Price of Admiralty* (New York: Viking, 1989), p. 276.

43. Thomas Clarkson, *The History of the Rise, Progress, and Accomplishment of the Abolition of the African Slave-Trade by the British Parliament*, 2 vols. (London: L. Taylor, 1808), p. 111.

44. Ibid., 29.

45. Hortense Spillers, "Mama's Baby, Papa's Maybe: An American Grammar Book," *Diacritics* 17, no. 2 (Summer 1987): 72.

46. Sharpe, *Monstrous Intimacies*, p. 3.

47. Olaudah Equiano, *The African: The Interesting Narrative of the Life of Olaudah Equiano* (London: Black Classics, 1998), p. 56.

48. https://spartacus-educational.com/USAS ships.htm [accessed March 2023].

49. Browne, *Dark Matters*, p. 49.

50. Ibid., p. 50.

51. Édouard Glissant, *Poetics of Relation*, trans. Betsy Wing (Ann Arbor: University of Michigan Press, 1997), pp. 169, 16.

52. Ibid., p. 33.

53. Ibid., p. 6.

54. Ruth Miller, *The Limits of Bodily Integrity: Abortion, Adultery and Rape Legislation in Comparative Perspective* (London: Routledge, 2007).

55. For a moving account of this logic, see Alice Walker, "The Right to Life: What Can the White Man Say to the Black Woman?" *Seattle Journal for Social Justice* 1, no. 1 (2002): 7–12.

56. Hartman, *Lose Your Mother*, p. 110.

57. Glissant, *Philosophie de la Relation* (Paris: Gallimard, 2009), p. 144–5.

58. Hartman, *Lose Your Mother*, p. 110.

59. Sharon Holland, *Raising the Dead: Readings of Death and (Black) Subjectivity* (Duke University Press, 2000), p. 6.

60. Sharpe, *Monstrous Intimacies*, p. 4.

61. Jennifer Morgan, *Labouring Women: Reproduction and Gender in New World Slavery* (Philadelphia: University of Pennsylvania Press, 2011), p. 56.

62. Holland, *Raising the* Dead, p. 6.

63. Abdul R. JanMohamed, *The Death-Bound-Subject: Richard Wright's Archaeology of Death* (Durham, NC: Duke University Press, 2005), pp. 2–3.

64. https://nytimes.com/2023/01/18/us/doula-black-women.html [accessed April 2023].

65. Sharpe, *Monstrous Intimacies*, p. 9.

66. Quoted in "Officers who Serv'd Several Years at Land and Sea," in *A Military Dictionary. Explaining All Difficult Terms in Martial Discipline, Fortification, and Gunnery*, third edition improv'd (London: J. Morphew Near Stationers-Hall, 1708), p. 246.

67. James Orchard Halliwell, *A Dictionary of Archaic and Provincial Words: Obsolete Phrases, Proverbs, and Ancient Customs from the Fourteenth Century*, vol.

2: J–Z, tenth edition (London: John Russell Smith, 1881), p. 787.

68. William Henry Smith, ed., Sir Edward Belcher, *The Sailor's Word-Book: An Alphabetical Digest of Nautical Terms* (London, Glasgow, and Edinburgh: Blackie and Son, 1867), p. 645.

69. See the famous customs of Welsh spoon.

70. Harney and Moten, *Undercommons*, 91.

71. Gargi Bhattacharyya, *Rethinking Racial Capitalism: Questions of Reproduction and Survival* (London: Rowman and Littlefield, 2018), p. 18.

72. Audre Lorde and Adrienne Rich, "And Interview with Audre Lorde," *Signs* 6, no. 4 (Summer 1981): 713–36.

73. "Ephemera as Evidence: Introductory Notes to Queer Acts," *Women & Performance: A Journal of Feminist Theory*, 8, no. 2 (1996): 5–16.

74. Spillers, "Mama's Baby, Papa's Maybe: An American Grammar," p. 76.

75. Hortense Spillers, "The Politics of Intimacy," *Black, White, and in Color: Essays on American Literature and Culture* (Chicago: University of Chicago Press, 2003), p. 104.

76. Stephanie Smallwood, "Politics of the Archive and History's Accountability to the Enslaved," *History of the Present* 6, no. 2 (2016): 126. For how she does this, see her book, *Saltwater Slavery: A Middle Passage from Africa to American Diaspora* (Cambridge, MA: Harvard University Press, 2007).

77. Dionne Brand, *A Map to the Door of No Return: Notes on Belonging* (Toronto: Doubleday Canada, 2001), p. 21.

78. Munoz, "Ephemera as Evidence," p. 6.

79. Jarrett Hugh Brown, "Black Masculinities as Marronage: Claude McKay's Representa-

tion of Black Male Subjectivities in Metropolitan Spaces" (doctoral dissertation, College of William & Mary, 2011), https://dx.doi.org/doi:10.21220/s2-shen-wn74 [accessed December 2022]; Ronald Bancroft Cummings, "Queer marronage and Caribbean Writing" (doctoral dissertation, University of Leeds, 2012).

80.   Édouard Glissant, *Caribbean Discourse: Selected Essays* (University Press of Virginia, 1992), pp. 16, 26.

81.   Omise'eke Natasha Tinsley, "Black Atlantic, Queer Atlantic: Queer Imagings of the Middle Passage," *GLQ: A Journal of Lesbian and Gay Studies* 14, no. 2–3 (2008): 196. See also, Tinsley, *Thiefing Sugar: Eroticism Between Women in Caribbean Literature* (Durham, NC: Duke University Press, 2010), p. 7.

82.   Ibid., pp. 191–2.

83.   Ibid., p. 192. Italics in the original.

84.   LaMonda Horton Stallings, *Funk the Erotics: Transaesthetics and Black Sexual Cultures* (Champaign: University of Illinois Press, 2015), p. xii.

85.   Treva B. Lindsey and Jessica Marie Johnson, "Searching for Climax: Black Erotic Lives in Slavery and Freedom," *Meridians* 12, no. 2 (2014): 170.

86.   Harris, "History, Fable and Myth in the Caribbean and Guianas," p. 159.

87.   See Elizabeth MacGonagle's "From Dungeons to Dance Parties: Contested Histories of Ghana's Slave Forts," *Journal of Contemporary African Studies* 24, no. 2 (2006): 254.

88.   Dionne Brand, *What We All Long For* (Toronto, Vintage, 2005).

89.   Dionne Brand, "Jazz," *Bread Out of Stone* (New York: Random House/Vintage, 1994), p. 161.

90. Brand, *What We All Long For*.

91. Stephanie L. Simek, Jerrold L. Belant, Brad W. Young, Catherine Shropshire, and Bruce D. Leopold, "History and Status of the American Black Bear in Mississippi," *Urus: International Association for Bear Research and Management* 23, no. 2 (2012): 159–67.

92. See his letter to Secretary of the Smithsonian Institution Charles D. Walcott in True, Webster P., "The Smithsonian Institution," in *Smithsonian Scientific Series*, (vol. 1, Smithsonian Institution Series, Inc., New York: 1938), p. 193.

93. Greg Grandin, *The End of the Myth: From the Frontier to the Border Wall in the Mind of America* (New York: Henry Holt and Company, 2019).

94. John S. Watterson, *The Games Presidents Play* (Baltimore: The John Hopkins University Press, 2002), p. 49.

95. See Sophie Lewis' book, *Full Surrogacy Now: Feminism Against* Family (London and New York: Verso Books, 2019).

96. See for example: https://cuddlist.com [accessed February 2023].

97. On the racist origins of the advertising industry, see McClintock, *Imperial Leather: Race, Gender, Sexuality in the Colonial Contest* (New York: Routledge, 1995).

98. See Justin Leroy's "Black History in Occupied Territory: On the Entanglements of Slavery and Settler Colonialism" *Theory & Event* 19, no. 4, (2016).

99. "White Ignorance," in *Race and Epistemologies of Ignorance*, eds., Shannon Sullivan and Nancy Tuana (Albany: State University of New York Press, 2007), p. 247.

100. Mahesh Rangarajan, *Fencing the Forest: Conservation and Ecological Change in India's Central*

Provinces, 1860–1914 (New Delhi, Oxford, and New York: Oxford University Press 1999), p. 145.

101. John M. MacKenzie, *The Empire of Nature: Hunting, Conservation, and British Imperialism* (Manchester: Manchester University Press, 2017), p. 80.

102. Nathan Mote, "The Forgotten Legend of Holt Collier," *The Heritage Post: Preserving American* Heritage, https://heritagepost.org/american-civil-war/the-forgotten-legend-of-holt-collier/

103. Jodi A. Byrd, *The Transit of Empire: Indigenous Critiques of Colonialism* (Minneapolis: University of Minnesota Press, 2011), p. xvii and Chapters 2, 3, and 5.

104. *Holt Collier Documentary Film*, Matthew's Film Company, 2017.

105. Simon Clay, "The (Neo)Tribal Nature of Grindr," in *Neo-Tribes: Consumption, Leisure and Tourism*, ed., Anne Hardy, Andy Bennett, and Brady Robards (Cham: Springer International Publishing, 2018), pp. 235–51. https://researchgate.net/publication/321712741_The_NeoTribal_Nature_of_Grindr [accessed March 2023].

106. Rebecca Popenoe, *Feeding Desire: Fatness, Beauty, and Sexuality among a Saharan People* (New York: Routledge, 2004).

107. R.W. Connell and J.W. Messerschmidt, "Hegemonic Masculinity: Rethinking the Concept," *Gender and Society* 19, (2005): 829–59; bell hooks, *We Real Cool: Black Men and Masculinity* (New York: Routledge, 2003).

108. *Totemism*, trans. Rodney Needham (Boston, MA: Beacon Books, 1963).

109. The area ranged from Mombasa through Kenya to Uganda and the Southern Sudan.

Roosevelt, many argue, helped sow the form of the great game parks of East Africa today.

110. Theodore Roosevelt, *African Game Trails* (New York, C. Scribner's Sons, 1910), p. 21.

111. Robin Pogrebin, "Roosevelt Statue to Be Removed from Museum of Natural History," *New York Times*, June 21, 2020.

112. Elizabeth Hanson, *Animal Attractions: Nature on Display in American Zoos* (Princeton: Princeton University Press, 2002), p. 106.

113. Ernst Bloch, "Pippa Passes," in *Traces*, trans. Anthony A. Nassar (Redwood City: Stanford University Press, 2006), p. 61.

114. Salman Rushdie, "At the Auction of the Ruby Slippers," in *East, West: Stories* (London: Jonathan Cape, 1994), p. 101.

115. https://faroutmagazine.co.uk/conspiracy-theory-death-of-sam-cooke/ [accessed March 2023].

116. Jennifer Nash, *The Black Body in Ecstasy: Reading Race, Reading Pornography* (Durham, NC: Duke University Press, 2014), pp. 11, 4.

117. John Nguyet, "Queer Figurations in the Media: Critical Reflections on the Michael Jackson Sex Scandal," *Critical Studies in Mass Communication* (June 1998): 161.

118. Nash, *The Black Body in Ecstasy*, 150.

119. Sabrina Strings, *Fearing the Black Body: The Racial Origins of Fat Phobia* (New York: NYU Press, 2019), p. 6.

120. Ibid., p. 91.

121. Cited in Lynne Joyrich's "Queer Television Studies: Currents, Flows, and (Main)streams," *Cinema Journal* 52, no. 2 (Winter 2014): 133.

122. Jackie Wang, *Carceral Capitalism* (Cambridge, MA: Semiotext(e), 2018); Hortense Spillers, "Mama's Baby, Papa's Maybe: An American Grammar Book," p. 74.

123. Sunera Thobani, *Exalted Subjects: Studies in the Making of Race and Nation in Canada* (Toronto: University of Toronto Press, 2007). While Thobani doesn't use the language of necropolitics, she has a similar assessment of the welfare state apparatus and focuses on families and racialized mothering (as failed mothering that needs intervention).

124. Spillers, "Mama's Baby, Papa's Maybe," p. 65.

125. Ibid., p. 259.

126. Daniel Moyniha, *The Negro Family: The Case for National Action* (Washington, DC: Office of Policy Planning and Research, US Department of Labour, 1965), p. 5.

127. Spillers, "Mama's Baby, Papa's Maybe," p. 66.

128. Ibid., p. 80.

129. Carol B. Stacks, *All Our Kin: Strategies for Survival in a Black Community* (New York: Harper and Row, 1975).

130. Ibid., p. 22.

131. Julian Le Grand and Bill New, *Government Paternalism: Nanny State or Helpful Friend?* (Princeton: Princeton University Press, 2015).

132. http://archive.spectator.co.uk/article/3rd-december-1965/11/70-mph [accessed April 2023].

133. Jean Binta Breeze, "The Arrival of Brighteye," in *The Arrival of Brighteye and Other Poems* (London: Bloodaxe, 2000), p. 54.

134. Paul Gilroy, *There Ain't no Black in the Union Jack: The Cultural Politics of Race and Nation* (Chicago: University of Chicago Press, 1991).

135. Lisa Lowe, *The Intimacies of Four Continents* (Durham, NC: Duke University Press, 2015), p. 36.

136. Ibid., p. 21.

137. https://cuddlist.com/about-us/ [accessed February 2023].

138. https://cuddleparty.com/about-cuddle-party-inc/ [accessed February 2023].

139. Sara, Lloyd, "Cuddling Up to Communicate: Companies Must Learn to Challenge Assumptions and Extend Their Reach, Insights and Capabilities in the Digital Environment," *The Bookseller*, no. 5567 (March 15, 2013): 17, *Gale Literature Resource Center*, link.gale.com/apps/doc/A323658202/LitRC?u=ubcolumbia&sid=summon&xid=040e22a2 [accessed January 2023].

140. Paula Chakravartty, and Denise Ferreira da Silva, "Accumulation, Dispossession, and Debt: The Racial Logic of Global Capitalism— An Introduction," *American Quarterly* 64, no. 3 (2012): 361–85.

141. Debt Collective, *Can't Pay, Won't Pay: The Case for Economic Disobedience and Debt Abolition*, (Chicago: Haymarket, 2020).

142. https://ispot.tv/ad/7hMF/strayer-university-change-featuring-steve-harvey

143. https://youtube.com/watch?v=voyB4jPsp9E

144. Suzanne Khan, Mark Huelsman, and Jen Mishory, "How Student Debt and the Racial Wealth Gap Reinforce Each Other," The Roosevelt Institute, 2019. https://rooseveltinstitute.org/wp-content/uploads/2020/07/RI_Student-Debt-and-RWG-201909.pdf [accessed December 2023].

145. Anna Louie Sussman, "The Effects of For-Profit Colleges on Student Outcomes and Debt," National Bureau *of* Economic Research, (December 12, 2018), https://nber.org/digest/dec18/effects-profit-colleges-student-outcomes-and-debt [accessed April 2023].

146. Paulo Freire, *Pedagogy of the Oppressed* (New York: Continuum, 1989).

147. Paulo Freire, *Pedagogy of Freedom: Ethics, Democracy, and Civic Courage* (Lanham, MD and Oxford: Rowman and Littlefield, 2001).

148. Ibid., 83.

149. https://help.senate.gov/imo/media/for_ profit_report/PartII/Vatterott.pdf [accessed April 2023].

150. https://kansascity.com/news/local/article 321331.html [accessed March 2023].

151. Amanda Sakuma, "Michael Brown's Bright Future, Cut Short," *MSNBC* (August 21, 2014), https://msnbc.com/msnbc/michael-browns-future-cut-short-msna395746 [accessed March 2023].

152. https://harvardlawreview.org/print/vol-128/ policing-and-profit/ [accessed March 2023]; Wang, *Carceral Capitalism*.

153. Charles H. F. Davis III, Jalil Mustaffa Bishop, Kyah King, and Ayan Jama, *The Legislation, Policy, and the Black Student Debt Crisis: A Status Report on College Access, Equity, and Funding a Higher Education for the Black Public*, National Association for the Advancement of Colored People, 2020, p. 6.

154. Paula Chakravartty and Denise Ferrarie da Silva, "Accumulation, Dispossession, and Debt: The Racial Logic of Global Capitalism— An Introduction," *American Quarterly* 64, no. 3 (2012): 364.

155. Michael Dawson, "Black Politics and the Neoliberal Racial Order," *Public Culture* 28, no. 1 (2015): 38–40; American Civil Liberties Union, "Justice Foreclosed: How Wall Street's Appetite for Subprime Mortgages Ended Up Hurting Black and Latino Communities," American Civil Liberties Union, 2012.

156. Michelle Alexander, *The New Jim Crow: Mass Incarceration in the Age of Colorblindness* (New York: The New Press, 2010); Alexes Harris. *A Pound of Flesh: Monetary Sanctions as Punishment for the Poor* (New York: Russell Sage Foundation, 2016).

157. Arpit Gupta, Ethan Frenchman, and Douglas Swanson, "The High Cost of Bail: How Maryland's Reliance on Money Bail Jails the Poor and Costs the Community Millions," Maryland Office of the Public Defender, 2016, p. 4, https://ma4jr.org/wp-content/uploads/2014/10/High-Cost-of-Bail.pdf [accessed August 2023]; Micoll Seigel, "Hypothecation: Debt Bondage for the Neoliberal Age," *Transition: An International Review* 114, no. 1 (2014): 139.

158. Seigel, "Hypothecation," p. 136.

159. Hartman, *Scenes of Subjection: Terror, Slavery*.

160. Patricia Hill Collins, "Mammies, Matriarchs, and other Controlling Images," *Black Feminist Thought: Knowledge, Consciousness, and the Politics of Empowerment* (London: Routledge, 1990), p. 73.

161. Spillers, "Mama's Baby, Papa's Maybe," p. 71.

162. https://edition.cnn.com/2021/05/16/politics/biden-welfare-queen-blake/index.html [accessed March 2023].

163. William C. Anderson, *The Nation on No Map: Black Anarchism and Abolition* (Chico, CA: AK Press, 2021).

164. Sianne Ngai, *Our Aesthetic Categories: Zany, Cute, Interesting* (Cambridge, MA: Harvard University Press, 2012), p. 85.

165. *On Property: Policing, Prisons, and the Call for Abolition* (Windsor, ON: Biblioasis Publishing, 2021), p. 20.

166. Nahum Dimitri Chandler, *X—The Problem of the Negro as a Problem for Thought* (New York: Fordham University Press, 2014), p. 4.

167. Gilles Deleuze, *The Fold: Leibniz and the Baroque*, trans. Tom Conley (London: The Athlone Press, 1993), p. 37.

168. Ibid., p. 6.

169. Bernard Tschumi, *Architecture Concepts: Red is Not a Colour* (New York: Rizzoli, 2012), p. 356.

170. Sara Ahmed, *Strange Encounters: Embodied Others in Post-Coloniality* (London and New York, 2000), p. 5.

171. "Review of Deadly Force Incident: Tamir Rice," http://prosecutor.cuyahogacounty.us/pdf_prosecutor/en-US/Tamir%20Rice%20Investigation/Crawford-Review%20of%20Deadly%20Force-Tamir%20Rice.pdf [accessed August 2023].

172. *Los Angeles Times* Staff, "Hear the 911 Call About Tamir Rice: Gun is 'Probably Fake,' Caller Says," *Los Angeles Times*, November 26, 2014, https://latimes.com/nation/nationnow/la-na-nn-tamir-rice-911-call-20141126-htmlstory.html [accessed November 2022].

173. Crystal Lynn Webster, *Beyond the Boundaries of Childhood: African American Children in the Antebellum North* (Chapel Hill: University of North Carolina Press, 2021), p. 146.

174. Frank Chin and Jeffery Paul Chan, "Racist Love," in *Seeing through Shuck*, ed., Richard Kostelanetz (New York: Ballantine Books, 1972), p. 65.

175. "The Controversial Origin of Asian American Studies," *Paris Review*, January 15, 2020.

176. Chin and Chan, "Racist Love," p. 65.

177. Sianne Ngai, *Our Aesthetic Categories*, p. 5.

178. Adam Flemming, "David Cameron and Hug-a-Hoodie Phrase History," June 6, 2011. https://bbc.com/news/av/uk-politics-13669826 [accessed December 2022].

179. Ibid.

180. Mimi Thi Nguyen, "The Hoodie as Sign, Screen, Expectation, and Force," *Signs: Journal of Women in Culture and Society* 40, no. 4 (2015): 792.

181. Harney and Moten, *The Undercommons*, pp. 117–18.

182. Eduardo Galeano, *The Book of Embraces*, trans. Cedric Belfrage and Mark Schafter (New York: W. W. Norton, 1992), p. 135.

183. Stephano Harney and Fred Moten, *All Incomplete* (Wivenhoe: Minor Compositions, 2021).

184. Daniel Coleman, "Grammar Lesson," unpublished poem.

185. Brand, *A Map to the Door of No Return*, p. 25.

186. Rinaldo Walcott, *On Property: Policing Prisons, and the Call for Abolition* (Windsor, ON: Biblioasis Publishing, 2021), p. 64.

187. Ibid., p. 81.

188. Sara Ahmed, *Willful Subjects* (Durham, NC: Duke University Press, 2014), p. 3.

189. Ibid., pp. 1–2.

190. Matt Taibbi, *I Can't Breathe: A Killing on Bay Street* (New York: Spiegel & Grau, 2017), p. 55.

191. Stuart Hall, Chas Critcher, Tony Jefferson, John N. Clarke, and Brian Roberts, *Policing the Crisis: Mugging, the State, and Law and Order* (London: Macmillan, 1978), p. 394, emphasis mine.

192. This chapter is inspired by the capacious methodologies that animate the essay genre in Black and Caribbean studies. See Katherine

McKittrick's *Dear Science and Other Stories* (Durham, NC: Duke University Press, 2021), for the attention she pays to the science-based thinking in Black studies; read any essay by Marlene NourbeSe Philip (check out my favourite, *A Genealogy of Resistance—and Other Essays* (Toronto: Mercury Press, 1997), and Dionne Brand (*Bread Out of Stone: Recollections, Sex, Recognitions, Race, Dreaming, Politics,* Vintage Canada, 2019 [1998]), and Alexis Pauline Gumbs (*Undrowned: Black Feminist Lessons from Marine* Mammals (Chico, CA: AK Press, 2021), and essays by Ferreira da Silva, Édouard Glissant and Kamau Brathwaite and Aimé Césaire to experience the range of experiments they mobilize to teach us how to think collaboratively. I owe the poetics of affiliation that undergirds my writing and thinking to them.

193. Kamau Brathwaite, *ConVERSations with Nathaniel Mackey* (New York: We Press, 1999); Elizabeth Freeman, "Time Binds, or, Erotohistoriography," *Social Text* 23, nos. 3–4 (Fall–Winter 2005): 57–68.

194. Kamau Brathwaite, "Caribbean Culture: Two Paradigms," *Missile and Capsule,* ed., Jurgen Martini (Bremen, Germany: University of Bremen, 1983), p. 42.

195. Curdella Forbes, "The End of Nationalism? Performing the Question in Benitez-Rojo's 'The Repeating Island' and Glissant's 'Poetics of Relation,'" *Journal of West Indian Literature* 11, no. 1 (November 2002): 20.

196. As examples, see how in Frantz Fanon's *Black Skin White Masks,* Aimé Césaire's *Negritude,* Édouard Glissant's *Poetic of Relations,* their geopoetics mobilizes the dialectic to address

specific concerns in particular regions of the Caribbean, moving their work beyond dialectical thinking.

197. Brathwaite, "Caribbean Culture: Two Paradigms," p. 42.

198. Ibid.

199. Nathaniel Mackey, "An Interview with Edward Kamau Brathwaite," *Hambone* 9, (1991): 44. emphasis mine.

200. Brathwaite, *ConVERSations with Nathaniel Mackey*, p. 34. emphasis in original.

201. Frantz Fanon, *The Wretched of the Earth* (Harmondsworth: Penguin, 1963), p. 311.

202. Phanuel Antwi, "On Labor, Embodiment, and Debt in the Academy," *a/b: Auto/Biography Studies* 33, no. 2 (2018): 301–26.

203. Cornelius Castoriadis, "Window into Chaos," trans. Andrew Cooper, *Thesis Eleven* 148, no. 1 (2018): 78.